Rudolf Eickemeyer

Letters From the Southwest

Rudolf Eickemeyer

Letters From the Southwest

ISBN/EAN: 9783337005207

Printed in Europe, USA, Canada, Australia, Japan

Cover: Foto ©ninafisch / pixelio.de

More available books at **www.hansebooks.com**

LETTERS

FROM THE SOUTH-WEST

BY

RUDOLF EICKEMEYER

ILLUSTRATED BY E. W. DEMING

1894

THE letters have to speak for themselves, **but I have something to say about the illustrations.** I can pronounce all **true to** life except **two, the frontispiece and another, representing my partner on horseback. I did not see myself when mounted, and am therefore unable to** judge whether the artist **succeeded** in making a true **likeness.** The picture **of** the horse is a faithful one, but I have some doubts as **to the speed at which he seems to move.** If the artist intended to illustrate my feelings, **I think he is very nearly right, for I felt as if the horse** was galloping when **my companion said he walked.** Of the other picture, I can only say that I **was not present** on the occasion depicted. **I must have been at the** hotel writing letters when **the artist sketched the figure from life.**

THE AUTHOR.

LETTERS FROM THE SOUTHWEST.

I.

EL PASO, TEXAS, *February* 12, 1893.

MY DEAR MR. GORTON:

AFTER a long and cold trip through the "Sunny South" (snow eight inches in Atlanta, Ga., and more or less all the way to New Orleans), I landed in this place, by way of San Antonio, Texas, nearly two weeks ago.

I had left home with my son Carl during a heavy snow-storm, and this storm followed, or, rather, advanced, before us all the way to and beyond Mobile.

As luck would have it, the heating pipes in our sleeper burst before we left Jersey City, and we made the trip to New Orleans in a refrigerator car instead of the comfortably warmed "Pullman" for which we had paid.

The trip through Virginia, North and South Carolina, Georgia, and Alabama was anything but interesting. The country was covered with snow, and might as well have been in the northern part of New York, near the lakes, as in the South.

When we approached Montgomery the train passed through cedar swamps for hours, and for the first time we saw trees draped with Florida moss. At Westport we made our first acquaintance with the turkey buzzard, and it looked as if these birds knew that things were not as they should be. They would take a lazy flight upward, and a short view of the surroundings, which seemed to be unsatisfactory, and then perch on the fences and out-houses near the station.

We arrived at New Orleans twenty hours behind time and thoroughly disgusted with our experience. Our search after sunshine, so far, had not been a success.

New Orleans, with its long line of wharves loaded with cotton bales, sugar hogsheads, and other merchandise, piled tier upon tier, looked like an industrious place. But the French market, with the French and Spanish creoles and the negroes of all shades, made a strange picture for an American city.

Our stay there extended over a week, and what amused me more than anything else was that every one we met insisted that we must see the burying-grounds. Well, they were interesting enough; all the *burials* are above ground in sepulchral structures highly ornate. But to send a visitor, who has left home to restore his health, all over the city to see how New Orleans takes care of its dead, did not strike me as a very judicious move.

Our trip to San Antonio took us over a plain that was well cultivated in parts, and contained here and there a thriving village; but the vegetation constantly reminded us that we were going south. Along the fences were large cacti, and occasionally a Spanish "bayonet." We passed by large grain fields and cotton plantations, and in one of the latter saw a gang of convicts in striped suits hard at work, while mounted men, armed to the teeth, guarded them.

At some station along the route a gentleman left our car and forgot to take his satchel. The trainman who found it opened it to see if he could find a clew to the owner, and what do you think it contained? A shirt, a paper collar, and a six-shooter. Another proof that we were going south.

In San Antonio we saw the Alamo, where Davy Crockett and his compatriots held a whole Mexican army at bay; San Pedro Springs, in the Park, and the springs which are the fountain-head of the San Antonio River; some old churches, and a post where the United States have a garrison of fifteen hundred soldiers.

We left San Antonio for El Paso after a week's visit, and I must relate what induced us to come here. The fog and smoke that characterized New Orleans was only a little less dense in San Antonio, and as it did not agree with me, we partly concluded to go to Southern California. Then some of our friends suggested El Paso.

But El Paso was an unknown region, and our inquiries elicited no reliable information; so I requested Carl to go to some public library and look the place up in an encyclopædia. When he came back to the hotel he reported that El Paso was a town on the border of Mexico, having forty-five hundred inhabitants, half of whom were barbarous natives.

On the strength of this description we bought our tickets, and after a ride of twenty-four hours through a real desert, our train following the picturesque cañon of the Rio Grande a good part of the way, we landed here, as stated above, nearly two weeks ago. And I was surprised when I found, instead of the town described in the encyclopædia, a well-regulated American city, with churches and schools, and the schoolmaster on top.

El Paso is located in what looks to a stranger like a desert; and so it is unless water is obtainable for irrigation, and that seems to be the question of greatest importance to the city.

There is a high-school here with eighty-five pupils, and in this, as in the other schools, the rooms seem to be as well equipped as ours.

I have not had the ambition yet to visit all of the schools, but without doubt will do so before I get away. Besides the high-school there are three others (including one for Mexican and another for negro children), all under one superintendent and all in good buildings. Please get me excused for another month from the meetings of the Board of Education, as I intend to gather a whole lot of information on school-keeping while on my travels. I think this should be considered as an equivalent for regular attendance at the meetings of the Board.

The climate here is excessively dry, not more than six inches of rain-fall per annum; but for the last two years *no rain* has fallen in this section.

II.

El Paso, Texas, *March* 1, 1893.

I RECEIVED your letter yesterday, and was struck by the closing remarks about water and its uses, and especially by the suggestion that, where water is so precious, it would be unfair for a visitor to diminish the supply by drinking it. When I left home I had a sort of a notion that I might land somewhere where the water was scarce or bad, and so I ordered a supply of cigars and "Blue Grass" to be sent forward.

I have found since that it was the best thing I ever did. You see, great minds run in the same groove; by intuition I had done what you suggested after you heard of the scant rainfall in the section I now inhabit.

It may interest you to hear something about this part of "Uncle Sam's farm." El Paso is, as you know, in the State of Texas, and a mile or so from the Rio Grande. On the opposite side of the river is the Mexican town of El Paso del Norte, or, as it is now called, Juarez. It is necessary to keep this in mind to understand the condition of things on this side. To give you an idea how El Paso appears to a stranger, I must describe it as I gradually saw it.

I am lodged at the Vendome, an American hotel, and the best in town. We landed here at about nine o'clock in the morning, just four weeks ago to-day, and I had my first view of the place—bathed in sunshine under a cloudless sky—when I looked out of the window of my room. I had found sunshine at last. Right in front of the hotel is the Plaza, a sort of park covering four squares. This Plaza is daily filled with people, mostly from the North, who come here to mend their lungs. "Lungers," they call them here for short. You remember you once found me counting up the ages of my ancestors, to find out how near to the average I had arrived. Well, a walk on the Plaza on a sunny day—and six out of seven are sunny—is about as cheerful an occupation as that you found me at.

But to return to the original subject, namely, the description of the town. I must say that it looked on that morning as pleasant as any place I had seen. The Plaza has a fountain in the centre, and a sign on one side says: "Don't disturb the alligators." I have circled around the basin almost daily, but have not had the pleasure yet of seeing their open countenances; so that sign may be a deception and a fraud. On the left, and about the middle of the square, "Uncle Sam" has put his Federal building, containing the post-office, custom-house, and courts, and the flag is flying all day; so you feel at home, anyhow, no matter how strange the surroundings may seem.

The next building is a large business block, built of brick; and in the top story "Uncle Sam's" weather clerk has his roost. The wind-gauge and weather-vane crown the roof of this building, and, as I have a full view of them from my room, I have become an expert on the wind. By simply looking from my window I can tell where it comes from, and by the speed of the whirligig I can tell how fast it blows. There is also a registering thermometer on top, and regularly, at six o'clock in the evening, an attendant climbs a ladder to take the reading, and this reading is telegraphed to Washington to serve as part of the data for predicting the weather. Of course I had to climb up and investigate the method of observation, and while there I had a pleasant chat with the attendant. So, when for a number of days we had bad weather, I took the liberty of requesting that, as he had so little to do, he would furnish us a better article; and he did.

It seems that El Paso is out of the range of the storms, which form either in the Gulf of Mexico or in the Rocky Mountains. It is a sort of island, having a climate of its own, and, consequently, the observations taken here bear very little relation to the storms at the North. Still, the temperature depends in a measure, though not invariably, upon the quantity of snow on the plains. The other day the temperature here was ten degrees lower than at one hundred miles north or east of us, showing the climatic isolation of El Paso.

Now, to continue the description of the buildings around the Plaza, we have next to the post-office an *adobe* house. These *adobes* have few windows but many doors, and when I first saw one in San Antonio I could not help thinking of some fort with a lot of cannon mounted on the ramparts. The houses are one story high. The walls extend two or three feet above the flat roofs. Every eight or ten feet around the building wooden leaders project a distance of from four to six feet. They carry the water, when it rains, away from the foundation, and look from a distance like guns for the defence of a castle.

When I suggested to the weather-clerk that it seemed a useless precaution to put these leaders on the houses, he told me that at times (not very often indeed) rain fell at the rate of two inches an hour, and without this way of carrying off the water these houses would be washed away. Facing the hotel, on the opposite side of the plaza, are the ruins of a hotel which was burned some time ago, and adjoining these is a livery stable one story high, built of sun-dried clay bricks, filling the space to the next corner. The railroad runs along the fourth side of the plaza, thus completing the square.

Behind the buildings on the south side of the Rio Grande you see mountains, and at the west another range. Facing you is what they call the *Mesa*. I believe this is the Spanish for table, and should mean tableland. This is a deception; it is composed of a succession of hills and gullies, which look as if the rains of heaven had washed them out yesterday, but not a drop of water is in them. I am told that the sluggish stream is called the Rio *Grande* because at times its bed, which is one-eighth of a mile wide, is covered with water.

I don't know whether you have ever seen a "sage-brush" desert. Imagine a number of hills of pure, unadulterated loose sand, here and there a green bush or a cactus plant. Then imagine the same conditions as far as the eye can reach, with mountains from one thousand to fifteen hundred feet above the plain on either hand, enclosing an area about thirty-five miles long by eight or ten wide, stretching from El Paso toward the east, and you may get a sort of a notion of a desolation in which it would appear that no living being could exist; yet even here man does get a living in some way, such as it is.

El Paso is part Mexican and part American. The Mexicans and a great many of the Chinamen live in *adobe* houses; but there are a number of fine residences, built of brick, which contain all the modern improvements.

I have just reached the point where I might branch out and talk about the churches, schools, public halls, banks, and gambling houses, when I find I must stop for the day. There is going to be a drawing of the lottery in Juarez under the superintendence of the ex-Confederate Colonel Mosby, the one who had his field of action in the Shenandoah Valley during the late unpleasantness. He receives, I am told, eight thousand dollars a year for the use of his name and his personal attendance at the drawings. It would be too bad to miss that, so good-by, and the story is to be continued in our next.

III.

El Paso, Texas, *March* 4, 1893.

When I closed my last it was my intention to go to Juarez and see Colonel Mosby and the drawing of the lottery, but just as I had finished my letter to you and was ready to start, the Eastern mail came in, and I had to go right at it to answer my letters and get them away on that day. One of the advantages of this place is a regular mail service. There is a daily train each way, north, east, south, and west; and so your letters go, or *don't* go, if you happen to mail them at the right or wrong time.

This city has between ten and eleven thousand inhabitants, not counting the visitors; and to supply these people with drinks and an opportunity to get rid of any surplus cash, there are about twenty saloons, and to almost every saloon is attached a regular outfit for roulette, faro, sweat, crap, and keno. I put down these games by the names I have been told they go by. If I stay here some time longer I may be initiated into all the secrets of gambling, provided that the money holds out.

But I may as well tell this part of my story in the regular way. When it proved to be too late to go to Juarez, we organized a sort of an investigating party, or, **rather, a committee** on discovery ; and a little after two o'clock P.M. started **out to see** the town. There were six of us—a gentleman from Kentucky, another from Delaware, two young men from New Jersey, and my son. We had become acquainted during our stay here, and concluded that it might be as well to go in force. Now, when I speak of saloons, don't imagine that they are the ordinary kind of places where a man takes a drink. Oh, no ! They are carved and gilded, and everything is in first-class style, and their names are simply grand. El Paso Street is the leading business street, and as the saloons constitute the principal business the more stylish establishments are upon it. Come to think of it, they are as thick as the saloons on Main Street from the station **to** Getty Square, and as to the names, there is the " Drawing-Room," the " White House," the "Jewel," the " Tepee," the " Sachem," and so on.

We started on our expedition at the upper end of the street, which commences at the Plaza and extends, a straight, wide avenue, to Juarez. **On it** is the street-car line, **each car** being propelled by a mule as large as a good-sized goat, and the engineer, a Mexican, plies the whip incessantly.

To return, however, **to** our inspection. We had learned that the " Jewel " was the most stylish of the gambling-houses, and so we dropped in there first. The " bar " is about forty feet in length, and gotten up " regardless," as the **boys** say. This " bar," ornamented and embellished with statuary—lacking the conventional fig-leaf—is on the left ; and at **the end is a** black-walnut partition carved in the highest style of **art. We** passed through the door, and entered a room filled with **a** promiscuous crowd. There were Chinamen, Mexicans **(real** " Greasers "), negroes of all shades and colors, a few cow-boys, and some business men.

On the left a roulette game was in full play, and a solitary player was " bucking the tiger." He seemed to be in luck, and to be winning ; but as I did not understand the game, I could not follow his moves. Opposite the roulette another game was a-going which, I was told, was called crap— as mysterious as the other. This game was played with two dice. Adjoining this was a regular faro-table, and another, opposite to it, completed the outfit.

Now about the players. **At one** of the faro-tables I counted five Chinamen, two mulattoes, and one cow-boy ; at **the** other the cow-boys seemed to be in the majority, and some rough-looking " Greasers " completed the set. The faces of the players were a study. Some looked as if they did not care a fig how the game turned, while the faces of others expressed an excitement you seldom see. Of course, I did not stay long. It takes time to get used to such things, and I hope to be able to devote some to see it **out.** I am told that every saloon is equipped substantially in the same style; some even more elaborately, as far as gaming is concerned, than the "Jewel." This is all carried on in broad daylight, and, of course, all night. I first thought that these places were licensed. I have learned since that there is no such a thing; but the city of El Paso derives quite an income from these "dives," nevertheless. At the end of each month a collector goes around and fines (note this particularly) each keeper of a gambling-house (I think, fifty dollars), and if he cannot pay the fine the majesty of the law steps in and closes his place. This seems to me to be the finest illustration of the old saw, namely, "To beat the devil around the bush." I intended to continue a full description of our exploration that afternoon, but I find I have about used up my mental energy, and will have to stop and continue the description in my next.

I wish you would keep these letters for me. As I write, the subject grows on me, and if I stick to it I will have a story of El Paso second only to the "Mysteries of Paris," by Eugene Sue.

IV.

El Paso, Texas, *March* 4, 1893.

I GOT off one letter to you this morning and did not intend to write another; but even El Paso has a climate. Now the sun shines as brightly as it does on a clear day at home; but the wind blows at the rate, I should say, of twenty-five miles an hour, and the sandy plain and the hills furnish sand enough to make the atmosphere look hazy. Consequently I have to stay indoors. I will therefore proceed from where I left off.

Continuing our walk down El Paso Street, which contains a good number of brick blocks, interspersed here and there with one-story *adobe* houses, we reached what is called "Dobe-town." But again I have to stop in telling my tale of our exploration. As we arrived at the end of the business part, we had on our right the ruins of an *adobe* house; and thereby hangs a tale.

The city of El Paso has a great many Chinamen included in its inhabitants, and among these was an old crippled Chinaman, who was, as his countrymen said, "no good." The first or second week of my residence here I concluded to see some of the city authorities, and so my son Carl and I took a walk to the city hall. We found there a great crowd passing in and out of an engine-room of the Fire Department, and, on inquiring, ascertained that a roasted Chinaman was on exhibition. You may imagine how quickly I got out. The Chinamen who had to support the old fellow got tired of it; and when, about midnight, one of the city policemen (who was coming out of a saloon opposite the ruined hut) discovered the fire, he rushed over and kicked in the door and tried to pull the old man out. He could not do it, because the poor fellow was fastened down somehow, and the whole place was saturated with kerosene, so he had to let him burn up. This is, at any rate, the testimony produced before the coroner; and there the matter ended. The Chinaman was buried at the city's expense, and that is the whole story.

While I am at it, I may as well relate another incident characteristic of this place.

All the respectable citizens are, on occasions, armed with revolvers, and at times, when arguments get strong, they use them, although fisticuffs seem, to an extent, to take their place in the higher grades of society.

The other day a dispute arose between one of the best police officers of the city and an ex-sheriff. The lie was passed, and the sheriff let fly at the policeman with his fists. The latter evidently felt overmatched at that game, and, pulling his revolver, hammered away at the ex-sheriff's head until mutual friends (newspaper report) separated them. The sheriff's head was cut in half a dozen places, and he was taken to a drug store, where the cuts were sewed up and pronounced not dangerous. The policeman had to resign, and much regret was expressed that he had allowed his hasty temper to get the better of him. He was evidently looked upon as a highly efficient servant in the line of law and order.

Then, again, two gentlemen had a rather hot argument on some legal question, and to clear up the matter they came to blows. An unfortunate reporter of one of the dailies here got wind of it, and somehow must have reported the wrong man victor. Be that as it may, the wronged gentleman and the reporter met accidentally in the street, and a free fight was the result, until some mutual friends separated them. (You see the mutual friend cuts a great figure here.) Both rushed for a store to buy good stiff canes to go at each other again, but the mutual friend stepped in once more, and explanations and mutual apologies prevented any further contest. The papers said the next day that the combatants were going to keep the sticks as mementos of this chivalrous dispute.

But now I must give you a sketch of something that happened three weeks ago. About twenty miles from here some parties met. Two of them had a herd of cattle, about twenty in number; the other party, numbering three, contended that most of the cattle were stolen. Of course such an offence can only be washed out in blood, so both sides drew their revolvers and began to shoot. The two thieves were killed then and there. One had no less than six bullets in his chest; and the other, two in his head. The three men surrendered at once to the sheriff here in El Paso, and were released on five thousand dollars bail, and all three are about the city as unconcerned as anybody. It takes but a walk of about five hundred yards from the hotel to make their acquaintance.

V.

EL PASO, TEXAS, *March* 8, 1893.

I REGRET that I have not told my story in regular order, but I could not help it. When I saw the Chinaman's hut it started a new train of thought, and I had to run that down before I could go ahead. Now, to finish the description of that exploring expedition. I mentioned that we reached Dobe-town. Imagine eight or ten squares covered with mud houses, with señoras, some as dark as the darkest Indian you ever saw, performing their cooking and washing (such as it is) out of doors; dozens of young ones, half clad, and some almost *not* clad at all, running about playing, and you have a picture of this end of the town.

We followed the sandy avenue to the smelter, which has been shut down since the McKinley bill put a duty on silver ores from Mexico; passed by the square where the court-house stands, surrounded by a grass-plot with large cottonwoods here and there, and reached our hotel just in time for dinner.

Well, I am glad I have finished that trip, because I can go systematically at it to give you the sunny side of life in this place. To start, I will take you up on the Mesa or tableland, and show you a view that is as beautiful as any you may have seen. At the foot of the Mesa is El Paso. Close to the bluff are a dozen or more squares covered with trim brick dwelling-houses, each with its little garden and its cactus plants. A little farther east is the Plaza, enclosed on nearly three sides by solid buildings three or four stories high. El Paso Street, with its brick buildings, extends from the centre, south, over to Juarez, Mexico. And the American town, with its ten churches, four good school buildings, its county court-house—of which any city might be proud—and its city hall, clusters about the plain, covering an area of probably four square miles.

The streets are as level as a table and as straight as arrows. The sidewalks, of asphalt, are kept in good order, and as it does not rain very often it is easy to keep them. Outside of this part of the city (in which is the centre of travel, the railroads passing right through it) is the Mexican town. Scattered among the brick buildings of El Paso are numbers of *adobe* houses. Most of these are plastered over and have a clean and nice appearance. Surrounding the American city are hundreds—yes, I should say thousands—of *adobe* houses with just one, or at the outside two, rooms, all of them one story high, inhabited by Mexicans, negroes, and Chinamen.

The Rio Grande makes a great bend which, in a measure, puts El Paso on a peninsula. At present the water is so low that but little can be seen of the stream except its bed of white sand. A level plain stretches for

miles to the east and extends to the other side of the river, where El Paso del Norte lies before you as in a bird's-eye view. Its church, which is supposed to be three hundred years old, attracts your attention first; then the custom-house and post-office and the presidio, where the Mexican garrison guard their side of the border. A number of brick stores and a few brick dwelling-houses also appear above the *adobe* houses in which the Mexicans live; and as there are ten thousand inhabitants in the town you may imagine how much ground they cover.

All this country that you see is surrounded by hills, or mountains, from five hundred to fifteen hundred feet in height; they seem to form an irregular wall enclosing the wide plain. I spend a good deal of time up at the Mesa, and the oftener I go there the more impressive is the sight. El Paso—that is, the American town—is but a few years old. The first railroad entered it in 1879, I think, and all it is to-day has been created in these few years.

I wish I was able to do justice to the view; but as all my descriptive powers have been wasted on machinery of one kind or another, while I have not lost my ability to see and appreciate, my power of expressing my thoughts is but limited. So you must take the will for the deed and let your imagination fill in where my pen has left a blank.

I guess I will close right here, and when I feel like it again will give you some more.

There is a lot of material—cock-fights, bull-fights, etc.

VI.

EL PASO, TEXAS, *March* 12, 1893.

IN my last letter I tried to give a bird's-eye view of El Paso, and when I got through I felt that I was now ready to start in and tell you all about the good people. But I find myself on the wrong side yet. Every Sunday they have cock-fights in Juarez, and it would never do to go away from here and not see one. It would really be as bad, as the Germans say, "to go to Rome and not see the Pope." So last Sunday we started for Juarez to see the cock-fight, and I hope that next Sunday I will be able to see the bull-fight. But, to go at the subject, I have first to give you some geographical information.

As I said before, Juarez is on the other side of the Rio Grande, and is connected with El Paso by street-cars which pass over the river on two bridges. Going in one direction, they pass over the lower, returning, after a long detour through Juarez, over the upper bridge back to El Paso. As soon as the first bridge is crossed the car is stopped, and a Mexican custom-house officer passes through to inspect passengers and baggage. This inspection Carl calls "Bluff No. 41." I don't know why, but where "bluffs are trumps" (gambling-house slang), I suppose he has run up to that figure. The custom-house officer is a picturesque figure. With his broad *sombrero* trimmed with gold and silver braid, his short jacket and tight pantaloons, a cartridge-belt around his loins, and a silver-plated revolver in his belt, he looks like a robber in a Bowery theatre melodrama. (This is from hearsay, not from actual observation.) He rings the bell as he steps off of the rear platform, and away we go at full mule-speed into Juarez.

It being Sunday, everybody is in full dress. And right here I want to make an observation on something that, I think, is characteristic of the country. In other parts of the world the bright colors are worn by the better half of mankind; but here it is the opposite. All the señoras are dressed in sombre black, and the men in all the colors of the rainbow.

As we passed up the street, I noticed a Mexican dandy on horseback whom I had seen in El Paso at the hotel. Having acquired by long years of contact some Yankee inquisitiveness, I learned then that the hat (about two feet in diameter, more or less), of light color and trimmed with gold and silver braid, represented something like eighty dollars in value. The jacket and pantaloons, of the finest, softest leather I ever saw, and profusely ornamented with black braid, were worth about an equal amount; and the blanket which he wore gracefully thrown over one shoulder was of a striped pattern, varying from the deepest blue to pure white. I must confess I never saw a dress as picturesque as this, and I never imagined that any man could wear such a dress and not look ridiculous; and yet there he is, a hidalgo, every inch of him.

If I keep on at this rate over each Mexican we meet, I fear your patience will give out, because I suppose you want to hear about the cock-fight as much as I want to see it.

Our mule turned to the right, and we travelled along a street parallel to the Rio Grande (but about three-quarters of a mile away), and passed the American part of the town, where the German Jews monopolize all the business (the same as in middle Broadway, from Canal to Twenty-third Street, in New York). The custom-house is on the same street, and when our mule turns to the right again to return to El Paso, we will get out and be at a point where the old church is visible.

Of course the old church is the first thing to visit. It is built of sun-dried brick, and is at least three hundred years old. A square tower at the left and in front of the building has three bells, suspended in the most primitive manner, with ropes, to cross-beams. As we enter we see a bare floor—no pews or seats of any kind. The high altar fills an arched recess in the further wall, and to the right and left are altars of smaller dimensions. Along the walls on both sides are pictures of the saints, mostly cheap prints; but the ceiling of the church is the most attractive portion. It is formed of native timber, carved with elaborate designs. The dark wood of the ceiling and the dim light of the few windows seem to put you back some centuries, as you stay in the half-light on entering the door. Yet this picture of the church does not comprehend the scene.

2

Right in front of the church is a plaza, well laid out and planted with palms and cactus plants. The walks are lined with seats, on which old and young sit in the sun; and right in the middle, upon a stone pedestal, is a bust of Juarez, the president who established the Republic of Mexico on the ruins of the Empire of Maximilian.

In the rear of the church is, sad to relate, the lock-up; and a look through the gate at its inhabitants, who seem to have the freedom of the yard, destroys all the romance you may weave about this old part of El Paso del Norte. A Mexican soldier in dark blue uniform, himself as black as the ace of spades, walks to and fro in front of the gate, and a set of ragged urchins keep him company.

But when are you going to get at that cock-fight? I hear you ask, and I have only to say that we will come to it all in good time.

But right here is another interruption. As I told you before, directly in front of my window is the Plaza, and to-day (Sunday) a Mexican band from Ysleta, who wish to show their ability, are going to give us a concert. The hall-boy has just informed me that the concert will begin shortly, and as no seats are reserved I will have to close and try to get a good one.

VII.

EL PASO, TEXAS, *March* 13, 1893.

MY "Epistle to the Corinthians" was closed yesterday by the hall-boy, and I start in to-day on a subject which is more or less metaphysical. If you have taken the trouble to decipher my communications to you, I have no doubt you can read or have read between the lines a longing to get away from the bad people and get a hack at the good ones. It has been a puzzle to me ever since I started in, why I cannot get away from that end of the story. Now you know, and if you don't I will tell you, that whenever you want to investigate any subject, you want a good working theory to guide you.

I have for the last ten or fifteen years had a hobby. I was after magnets in all forms, and their application. I finally reached a point where I got the whole planetary system in the proper shape. The sun became an enormous dynamo; the planets were electric motors, and the whole system worked admirably and to my satisfaction.

When I first realized that, somehow or other, I could not get away from the end of the problem I had in hand, I looked around to see if there were not some good and sufficient reason for the attraction which the shady side of life down here had for me. And you see, as soon as my thoughts had crystallized so that I knew it was attraction, the scales fell from my eyes.

Why, it was as plain as a pikestaff. Society in El Paso, and, for that matter, everywhere else, is just like a big magnet, the molecules of which group themselves regularly, the good people forming one pole, say the north, and the bad ones the south pole; and between the two poles the rest of humanity are stratified in proper layers.

Now, suppose you take two magnets and bring poles of like denomination near each other, they repel; while, when poles of unlike denomination are brought together, they are attracted. Now here you have at once a clear and forcible explanation of all my troubles. The greasy Mexican who gathers cigar stumps regularly every day in front of the hotel and on the Plaza, or a gambling Chinaman at the faro-table—yes, even a bunco steerer—seems to be more interesting to me than all the good people I have so far met, and I see plainly that it will take all my time to follow out this line. And, on the whole, I don't know but it is as good a line as any. It reminds me of a German saw, which, badly translated, reads about as follows:

"The good in us, depend, my son,
Is but the bad we leave undone!"

VIII.

El Paso, Texas, *March* 16, 1893.

When I took you over to Juarez, a week ago last Sunday, I held out as one of the great inducements a cock-fight which was to take place. I got you over all safe on the International horse-car line, propelled by mules, and, if I remember rightly, left you in front of the lock-up. Well, I have now made up my mind that you shall see that cock-fight with your mind's eye—if my pen holds out to describe it. When we left the old Mexican cathedral, we turned to the right and found in the rear the aforementioned lock-up; and as we passed on we came to a building which, in a rough way, resembles a circus. This building is the Plaza del Toros, or, in plain English, the bull-ring. Now, if I was not in a hurry to get to the cock-fight, I might take the time to describe all the arrangements provided for this great national game of all the Spaniards and their descendants; but I will leave this until I have had an opportunity to judge for myself of the valor of the matadors who ride on blindfolded horses and kill innocent bulls. As we pass on, leaving the old church and the Plaza on our left, we finally reach a one-story *adobe* building where the cock-pit is located. To give you a clear picture of the situation, I have to describe an *adobe* of the better type a little more clearly than I have done.

The one we are going to enter covers an area of about one hundred and twenty feet square. Imagine that the outside of this square, say twenty feet in width, is covered with a low building enclosing a yard eighty feet square. Within the inner walls is a row of rough columns supporting a roof which extends as far as the columns. This regular colonnade runs around the inside of the yard, substantially in the same manner as in the buildings unearthed at Herculaneum and Pompeii. There are few windows outside, and the rooms, dark ones at best, are lighted and entered from the yard.

Now, to get at the pith of the matter, we enter through a portico which leads from the street to the square yard referred to above, and in the centre we find a circular wall, built of sun-dried brick; it is about twenty feet in internal diameter, and about two feet high, rounded on the top. This circle has two openings, and is surrounded by another circle, about two feet high and flat on top; on this the spectators are seated.

To fill this inner and outer circle with actors and spectators would take a pen more pliable than mine, yet I will make the attempt.

When I speak of Mexicans, you must remember that they are of all kinds and types, from a tawny yellow, such as you see frequently in the Dago in the "promised land" (right behind my house), to the deep red of the Indian, and even as black as a Congo negro. And right here you have them all in a bunch. Then there are tourists representing all the States in and out of the Union. As a cosmopolitan crowd, there is nothing to beat it.

In the inner circle are a lot of Mexicans, each one having his fighting-cock tied to a string by a peculiar strap around one leg, and a lot of other roosters tied to sticks in the ground all over the yard. You may imagine that music is not missing. Each bird sends his note of defiance to every other, and sun-rise in a barnyard is nothing to the din that greets your ears. But the owners of the fowls are equally excited; bets have to be made, and to make bets the roosters have to be matched as nearly as possible; and it seems that weight is of as much importance in a cock-fight as in the prize ring, where human brutes fight for glory and cash.

Considerable time is thus consumed. But when the purses are made up and all the bets are made (and I tell you silver dollars seem to be plenty), the arena is cleared, and the preparations for the fight begin in earnest. You probably think, as I did, that the roosters fought each other with their natural weapons; but there you are mistaken. The owners of the cocks pick them up (and right here I may say that they seem to be as tame as kittens, and look as if they had been raised in the families of their owners with the children), and fasten to the left leg a curved knife, sharp as a razor and about four inches in length. I asked to see one of these "slashers," and when I felt the keen edge and saw the curved shape, I thought that Saladin's sword with which he cut the silken cushion must have furnished the pattern.

Everything being ready, the two roosters were held by their owners—or, I should probably say, their trainers—close enough for them to just reach each other, to show each, I suppose, his enemy. They were then released about four feet apart, and they flew together with such fury that both were knocked down. But they were up and at it, and, in less time than it takes to tell the tale, one of them lay dead. I must own up to a little squeamish-

ness (if that expresses it), and I intended to go and call it done. But, as I tried to explain to you in my last, I could not help owning up that there was a certain attraction that caused me to stay.

The preliminaries of the second fight were much like those of the first; but the fight itself lasted much longer and ended in one of the roosters running away. I was told that the death penalty was the least that this coward had to expect, but did not see it applied. I saw a third fight, and then left.

Now I must tell you something that may want deep thought. You know I have raised chickens for a good many years, and flatter myself that I am a pretty fair judge of roosters. I could not, therefore, resist the temptation to select the winning birds. Of course, I could not bet except in a mental way. I picked the winning birds in the first and second fights, and when the third fight came on, a gentleman from Kentucky who stops at our hotel said : " I bet you that white rooster will win." I examined the red rooster critically and concluded he would be the winner, and we bet, not mentally, but half a dollar a side, and my bird lost the fight. Now I wonder if this half-dollar dimmed my judgment. In the other bets I was above all feelings of self-interest, and I won, but here I lost. You would oblige me if you would try to solve this riddle for me. Some night when you are in a philosophical mood, you may find the key.

But I have something to say about the actors. It surprised me to see such eagerness in the lookers-on. Their faces showed an excitement you would scarcely expect in the countenances of people who hardly ever smile. Our white fellow-creatures seemed to partake of the excitement, and while the fight was going on you could have heard a pin drop. I left after the third fight, and don't think I will ever want to see another.

IX.

El Paso, Texas, *March* 17, 1893.

I suppose you noticed (that is, if you read my letter on the cock-fight) that while I took you along and showed all there was to be seen in the cock-pit, I forgot to take you back with me to El Paso. I felt disgusted with the brutal fight, and perhaps that bet may have had something to do with it. At any rate I forgot your presence and took the first mule train to get away. You would naturally expect that, under such circumstances, a stranger, like yourself, for instance, would want to use his time to see the town on his own hook ; and I will tell you what usually happens to the poor, unprotected foreigner who does the town in the manner suggested.

Of course, the first object to visit is the old church. While examining the tower with its three bells, a young gentleman steps up, and, looking with a great deal of interest at the tower, remarks : " Ah, well, I suppose this is the old church they talk so much about. Well, it *is* a curiosity ! Look at the ropes that hold the bells ! Why, they look a thousand years old instead of the two or three hundred years that they say is the age of the church !" Of course the stranger, say yourself, is pleased to find somebody who can talk his " lingo," and then the young man is evidently a tourist like yourself; he carries a summer overcoat on his arm, and casually informs you that he has an hour or two on his hands before his train starts for the East, or the West, and he thinks the best use he can make of this time is to see Juarez. The conversation then turns on the various objects in sight. The young man is exceedingly anxious to get your opinion on all there it to be seen, all is so new and strange, and so you stroll along. You see the bull-ring and cock-pit, and, having been there before, furnish your new friend with a lot of information. You talk of the habits of the Mexicans, etc., when your friend calls your attention to a sign on one of the best-looking *adobe* buildings on the Plaza—"El Nuevo Mondo" (The New World)—and remarks: "I suppose this is something of a real Mexican inn of the old style. I wonder what it looks like! Have you ever been inside of one?" You have not, so you conclude to just look in and get one of those celebrated Mexican cigars and a glass of native wine. Your new friend objects to letting you pay for it, and playfully suggests to follow the example of two Mexicans who are throwing dice for drinks. You see no harm in that, and throw and win. You have to give your friend revenge; the ball is started, and in fifteen minutes by the watch your quondam friend has captured all the loose cash you had about you and has disappeared from the scene.

I have no doubt that you think no man could furnish such a description unless he had lived through it, but you are mistaken. The second day after I landed here, and before I tried to see Juarez, I met an oldish sort of a gentleman (they call me *the* old gentleman) in front of the hotel, who was greatly excited. He had but just arrived, had been over to Juarez, and "dropped," as they say hereabouts, seventy-five dollars in the innocent way I have described above.

The oldish gentleman referred to is the gentleman from Kentucky who won the bet on the third fight in the cock-pit Sunday last.

X.

El Paso, Texas, *March* 22, 1893.

I HAVE hesitated for a day or two about sending you any more of my pen-pictures of the towns of El Paso, because I began to doubt whether these epistles were interesting enough to you to keep them out of the waste-basket.

But I felt encouraged to keep on when I saw in the *Statesman* that you had accepted the position of judge in the "gold prizes": to encourage home literature and improvement. You may consider my descriptions of

El Paso as negative contributions mainly. A good part of them can well serve to illustrate how not to do things, and that side of the question is in most cases as important as the opposite.

I do not submit my letters for their merits as literary productions, and I don't want you to apply any of the ordinary rules of grammar or orthography (I believe that is the way it is spelled), but to consider them from the standpoint of those learned men who for years have tried to improve (?) the spelling of the English language!

But this is to be considered only as a sort of an introduction to our next trip in El Paso proper, and I will lead you along substantially as I would take a stranger in hand to show him Yonkers.

As you know, my headquarters for the last two months have been in the

Vendome Hotel, and that is as good a place to start from on our present excursion as any other. We will start out and cross the Plaza, with its fountain in the centre and basin in which there are actually two alligators. You may remember that I expressed a doubt as to their existence in one of my first letters; but there they are as large as life (one about four feet six inches and the other four feet long), and as we pass they are basking in the sun. Now these animals are not at all frisky. I have watched them for hours and have never been able to detect any movement but the winking of one eye. What adds some interest to the scene is when some dog gets into their neighborhood, and then the whole crowd of people who, like the alligators, are basking in the sun on the seats that surround the basin, watch with a great deal of interest to see what may take place if the poor dog gets too close to the front end of the alligator. There is a tradition afloat that at some time a little dog had his nose pinched by one of the saurians, and, of course, everybody expects that this may happen again.

I very much doubt that any of the lookers-on would really wish to see a poor dog swallowed with hide and hair, and yet this expectation gives as peculiar a zest to the spectacle as a performance on the tight-rope so dangerous that the spectators may expect to see a neck broken at any time.

But, leaving the Plaza, we are soon on El Paso Street, the principal business street of the city. We pass on, looking to the right and left, and reach San Antonio Street, which terminates at El Paso Street and runs at right angles to it. On one corner is one of the three national banks, and on the other is the "Drawing-Room." To enable the passer-by to be sure of the functions of the "Drawing-Room," there is a sign crossing the whole broadside of the building on San Antonio Street with the legend inscribed: "This is a saloon." We pass on, however, and the second or third door from there we find ourselves in front of the finest saloon in El Paso, namely, the "White House." Its appointments are A No. 1, and the gentlemanly proprietor receives us, after we have entered, with distinguished honors. You know, he is a man of importance in this city, and no stranger who wants to be considered anybody will miss the opportunity to get an introduction.

While I am at it, I may as well interrupt our tour of inspection for a minute, and give you the true value of my friend, the proprietor of the "White House." I met him some time ago, in company with some gentlemen who, like myself, do not wish to consume what little drinking water there is in this section. He invited me to call at his place, and, of course, I did, and he showed me over the establishment—bar in front, gambling-room in the rear, and parlors up-stairs. I felt highly honored with my reception; but picture to yourself my surprise when, on St. Patrick's Day, a friend of the proprietor of the "White House" called on me at the hotel, and invited me to take a seat in one of the carriages that were to form a part of the procession. Such an honor could not be refused, and punctually at two P.M. I reported at the "White House." My friend, the proprietor, was to act as grand marshal, and I doubt if any marshal of France under the great Napoleon was ever dressed as grandly as he. He is a gentleman who stands six feet in his stockings, and, as he told me, weighs one hundred and ninety pounds. He is well proportioned, and, riding in the lead, formed a grand figure-head for the parade.

I must let you into the secret of this St. Patrick's parade. St. Patrick's Day had to be celebrated, and as real Irishmen are very scarce in this neighborhood, it would never have done to have the affair fail. Everybody had to step in and help out, and such Irishmen as Mr. O'Schmeckenbecker, Mr. O'Shulz, Mr. O'Muller, and Mr. O'Eickemeyer, decorated with green ribbons, and carrying green flags with the harp of Erin, did yeomen's service in honor of the patron saint of old Ireland.

The celebration was a complete success. It was led by the marshal and his staff; these were followed by the McGinty brass band, dressed in green coats and green hats. All the coaches in town followed—the mayor and aldermen, prominent citizens, and such strangers as were thought of importance enough (like a gentleman from New York and his wife, and myself, for instance).

The procession started from and wound up at the city hall; but the real centre was the "White House." All the participants took something before they started, and refreshed themselves again after the procession had finished. In the evening there was a grand supper and speeches, to which your humble servant had a cordial invitation; but, unfortunately, having taken a walk of about three and a half miles before dinner, and having undergone the exertions entailed on following the procession, and also in getting into and out of it, I had to stay at home and go to bed early.

From what I heard of those who were present, I should judge that, aside from the mental feast (the speeches, and so forth), the supper was supplied on the recipe of a friend of mine, who always insisted that a good meal should consist of one dollar's worth of eat and five dollars' worth of drink.

When I started in I expected to show you a good part of the city, but here I am. We have just walked one block on San Antonio Street, and have seen two of the important points, and I am all tired out and must close. I will promise faithfully, however, to carry you along at a ten-mile gait the next time, when I will call for you at the "White House," where I hope you will enjoy yourself until my next.

XI.

El Paso, Texas, *March* 23, 1893.

Yours of the seventeenth has just reached me, and I note with pleasure that Uncle Jacob is the new trustee. If good, solid, common sense is a desirable qualification, he has that in the highest degree.

Now, as to your flattering proposition to publish my letters in the *Statesman*, I don't see my way clear. When I first came here I had a notion to send to Mr. Oliver some of my views about matters and things hereabouts, and I actually started in and wrote a number of pages, when I got up a stump. I had to write a letter as if I was delivering a lecture before a class in a Sunday-school, and I gave it up in despair. The letters

I wrote you would be hardly suitable for publication, because when I wrote them I did not try to hide my leanings. You have undoubtedly heard of the saying of old Horace Greeley, when somebody asked him if his biography, which had just been published, was true. "True!" said he. "I would as soon walk up Broadway naked as to have **my true** biography published!"

When I tried to write **to** Mr. Oliver, I had to write **us if in** full-dress suit, my best manners ready at hand; while the letters I wrote you were, figuratively speaking, written in my shirt-sleeves, my boots on the table, puffing a cigar, a good glass of "Blue Grass" in, and another in sight.

A day or two ago I wrote you a treatise on a new theory, or, rather, **a** new philosophy on the good and the bad, and I have no doubt that after reading it you will take my view of my letters. If you edited them to make them suitable for the *Statesman*, you would have "to play Hamlet with Hamlet left out." And then, again, I may not get away from here for some time; and if, by some unforeseen circumstance, one of **the copies of** the *Statesman* should find its way down to El Paso, some of our best citizens might take exception to my views, and might feel tempted to use me as a target, a thing I should very much regret.

XII.

El Paso, Texas, *March* 26, 1893.

When I left you in the "White House," three or four days ago, I did not expect that your stay there would be such a lengthy one. Had I thought that I could not take up our tour until to-day, I might have taken you to the hotel with me, and given you three or four days to study "mine host" and his customers. We will do that some time later on, and will now proceed down San Antonio Street and see what is to be seen.

The "White House" is, as you may remember, on the left-hand side of the street, and diagonally opposite is the "Tepee," a fashionable resort in which the young bloods of our best citizens can be found. It has its gambling establishment in the rear, and posters inform visitors that keno is played every night.

While I think of it, I may as well refer to a little thing that happened in this place some time ago. A number of the sons of the same best citizens referred to before called at the "Tepee" late at night, or, more properly speaking, early in the morning. All were drunk, and the barkeeper, being sober, refused to sell them any more liquor; whereupon **the** young gentlemen drew their "guns," and a general shooting-match was in operation. Fortunately, no other damage was done than the smashing of looking-glasses, bottles, and so forth, for which an amicable settlement was made next day.

Adjoining this establishment is the "Kitchen," and this place is so characteristic that it deserves special notice. It is a restaurant kept, like most others in this city, by sons of the Chinese Empire. As you enter you see on your left a counter, behind which the cashier is seated. He is dressed in immaculate white; his pigtail is wound around his head in such an artistic way that it seems to form the edge of a black skull-cap, the black hair on his head, carefully drawn down, forming the crown. A row of tables extends through the middle of the room, and on each side are stalls in which parties of four can dine in private. The waiters are all Chinamen and are dressed like the cashier, and the whole place is as neat as a pin. The meals served are excellent, which is more than can be said of most of the places I have tried since I left home.

There are about a dozen establishments of this kind in the city that are principally patronized by visitors, as but few stay at the hotels for any length of time. In almost every private house are furnished rooms to let, and most of the invalids, after their arrival, select private rooms and take their meals at these restaurants.

But I see I have to get on, or we will never get through with our trip; and, by the way, I think I have found the reason why my letters get more long-winded the longer I keep at it. When I left home I did not take anything along to read during my absence. In New Orleans I found that I did not want to read newspapers all the time, and you may imagine my pleasure when I found, on a news-stand, a copy of Scott's "Ivanhoe" and another of "Kenilworth." I have read these two until I have "Ivanhoe" by heart and "Kenilworth" almost as well, and I think this fact accounts for a good deal of my composition, in so far as the minutiæ of description are concerned.

At this end of the block is the second of the National banks of this city, and on the opposite corner is the third. The next block starts in as the first one on El Paso Street did, namely, with a saloon. The one on El Paso Street bore the legend: "This is a saloon"; and the one on this corner—the "Castle"—has a sign of equal size and prominence: "This is the other saloon." It is not worth while to inspect them all; but we will pass on and simply read the signs. For a whole block, saloons and restaurants follow each other, and the sidewalk is filled with the customers of these places.

After we have passed this business block we find a number of brick buildings in which other kinds of trade are carried on, and the El Paso

Herald, one of the daily newspapers, stretches its sign in heavy gilt letters over the sidewalk. I may in time give you an introduction to the editor; but at present we have to pass on to reach the institution I have been anxious to take you to for some time.

As we turn to our right we see, on a wooden building one story high, and at the corner of the next street, a sign projecting some ten feet, with the inscription "Horse Restaurant." This is a most important institution. It is called the "corral," and all the ranch owners who visit the city to purchase supplies put up their "democrat" wagons, covered with canvas, and their ponies, horses, or mules, in the yard of this establishment. If you wish to see the regular Texas ranger, or the cow-boy unadulterated, this is your hunting-ground.

XIII.

El Paso, Texas, *March* 27, 1893.

I HAVE tried before to give you an insight into the social conditions of this place by roughly classifying the inhabitants into two sorts; namely, the good and the bad. But as I become more and more initiated, I find that I had done better had I said that there are two streams which flow alongside of each other, and only mingle in the gambling-houses—one representing the American, and the other the Mexican nationality—and then divided both in the manner above stated. Yet even this division would be faulty, for who can say what is good and what is bad?

I left you reading a sign on the corner of a street, and I will now take you into an establishment that forms the social and business centre of one class of the population of El Paso and the country that surrounds the city.

It is the "corral," the city centre of "ranger" life. A piece of ground about three hundred feet long and sixty or eighty feet wide has, on one side, a row of stalls in which the horses and mules are kept. The little frame building on the corner serves as a sort of office, and the "rangers" use the yard to keep their wagons in during their stay in town.

The proprietor of the Horse Restaurant, whom we met at the gate, takes us in hand, and, passing along in the rear of the open stalls, he shows us his stock. Small Texas ponies, called broncos, are in the majority, but here and there we see fine, broad-chested saddle-horses, and even Percherons, the elephants among the tribes of horses, represented. Two vehicles are drawn up on one side of the yard, true copies of the celebrated emigrant wagons that carried the early pioneers to the wild West.

The proprietor is an ex-Confederate soldier. He served during the war in one of the Texas regiments, and is a man between fifty and sixty years of age, with sandy hair and whiskers, and light gray eyes. If you ever go down East—say to Maine—and look at the farmer who has followed the plough all his life, you will find the perfect counterpart of the proprietor of the Horse Restaurant. His stooping shoulders, his sharp, bright eyes, his quiet and measured movements, reminded me so strongly of the "down-easter" that I could hardly believe my eyes when I found I had one of the Confederate heroes before me, who had served in the bloody fights of 1861 to 1865.

The conversation turned, of course, on horses and their good and bad points, and even the mules and "burros" were not forgotten. As we returned toward the gate, a young man stepped out of the office, and we were introduced to him as a ranchman from Hueco Tanks. He was a handsome young fellow, about twenty-five years of age, straight as an arrow, and dressed in Mexican style. A real sombrero ornamented with gold and silver braid covered his black hair, and his dark eyes and smooth face smiling under the broad brim made you pleased to shake hands with him. A black jacket, light-colored pantaloons, and an embroidered vest completed his suit. Two or three other gentlemen joined us, and the conversation turned from horses and burros to politics and the inauguration of Mr. Cleveland, and here the Eastern man had the advantage. None of those present had ever seen Washington, and a description of all the glories of our capital was listened to with both eyes and ears open by the enthusiastic Texans, who seem to look upon Mr. Cleveland as the great representative of the cause for which they had fought.

While the conversation was carried on behind the fence alongside of the gate, where a pile of old boards and some empty nail kegs served as seats for the audience, a new figure hove in sight. A regular cow-boy came riding into the yard. His horse, a good-sized Texan, showed some signs of travel, having made, in fact, forty-five miles that forenoon, and the rider, also, showed that out on the plains the sand had been drifting enough to cover him with dust.

A lariat was suspended from the pommel of his huge Mexican saddle; a broad-brimmed Stetson hat covered his head, and pantaloons tucked in his boots, together with extraordinarily large spurs, completed his outfit—not to forget a Colt's revolver suspended from a cartridge-belt that he wore around his waist. That finished the typical cow-boy of Texas and New Mexico. The gentleman had just come in from Hueco Tanks, a cattle range some forty-five miles from El Paso. After inquiries about mutual friends, the conversation turned on some local news that seemed to be

new to the cow-boy. I think it is thirty miles from here to Las Cruces, where, the day before, a young man, a student in a college at Las Cruces, had been shot dead by a cow-boy who was out of funds, and robbed of a few dollars. The reputation of the cow-boy was that of a bad man, and the question that was uppermost in all minds was whether he should be lynched, or hung in the regular way. Other matters of similar nature also came up and were talked of. When we withdrew, our friends invited us to repeat our visit whenever we had any leisure time on our hands, which we promised to do.

Now, as I have introduced to you the gentlemen who frequent the corral, I will give you something of their history. The proprietor of the Horse Restaurant owns a number of stock-ranges; he is a wealthy man. But some years ago he filled some of his neighbors with buckshot, and he has not visited that particular range for some time. It is said that the boys out there are lying in wait for him in the chaparral, and intend to give him a warm welcome should he venture there. As to the ranchman and the cow-boy, why, they are the two heroes who, four or five weeks ago, filled the two cattle thieves with bullets.

What I have related here is not, as you may imagine, a fancy picture. It is true to life, every line of it. You will agree with me that it would be ill-advised to publish my letters before I have put at least a thousand miles between myself and this glorious city of the North Pass.

XIV.

EL PASO, TEXAS, *March* 28, 1893.

YOU may have noticed that when I took you over to Juarez on a Sunday, some time ago, I kind of hustled you along. That is, we went over there in a sort of way to attract as little attention as possible. We sneaked into the cocking-main and got out in a sort of guilty way. It was on a Sunday, you know, and up our way we would not like to be seen doing such a thing.

Well, I have now resided here two months, breathing the free air of Western Texas and basking in the sunshine, and things and manners that at first seemed to go against the grain, as it were, seem now all regular and proper.

On our side of the Rio Grande, however, you are continually reminded of the Northern States and their Puritanical notions, and you have to go over to Juarez and leave the horse-car tracks to be transplanted into a new and strange world.

Sunday is the gala day of the Mexicans, and if you wish to see them at their best, you must go over on a Sunday afternoon, when all, old and young, are out of the *adobe* houses—the children playing in the sun, the young señoritas promenading the streets, and the señors walking about in their best attire.

Of course, the stores and *cantinas* (rum-shops) are open, and the venders of onions, peppers, and other Mexican delicacies carry on their trades on all the street corners. Among the Americans, the Mexicans have the reputation of having no enterprise; but before we get across the river I can furnish a proof that this is a mean slander. The usual way to go to Juarez is by horse-car, and then you are taxed ten cents; or, if you walk across one of the bridges of the International horse-car lines you are taxed two and a half cents. Now, don't you see that even here in the "Sunny

South" the grasping capitalist has spread his net to catch the pennies of the poor traveller. This exaction has led to a competition entirely creditable to our enterprising "Greasers." At the present stage of the river the water is not much deeper or wider than our own Nepperhan above the Moquette mills. Two stout, broad-shouldered Mexicans in high boots have started a ferry across the stream. For one and a quarter cents they carry men, women, and children over the river, and I tell you the enterprise pays big. A long string of passengers from both sides travel to and fro on the two-legged ferry-boats, and the wily capitalist is cheated out of his toll.

The path from the ferry leads to highly cultivated gardens in which, for weeks, the peach and apricot trees have been in full bloom, and pears and apples cast their snowy flowers on the ground. Every inch of land is cultivated, and the canals that serve to irrigate the land flow peacefully in all directions, carrying their life-giving moisture to tree and shrub.

The culture of grapes is rather singular. When I first came here I saw large pieces of ground that seemed to be covered with mammoth mole-hills. These hills, five or six feet apart, had a scrubby looking bush sticking out of the centre. The mole-hills have now disappeared. The soil, which had been piled around the vines to protect them, has all been spread out and levelled off, leaving only long furrows between the lines; into these the water has been turned to moisten the roots. The first leaves are now sprouting, and give a reddish-green cast to the tops of the vines.

It is a novel sight to a Northern man to see garden beds surrounded by boards that form basins to hold the water; and where no boards are used, the paths are raised above the beds to make dikes for the miniature lakes in which vegetables and flowers are planted and raised.

The whole country around Juarez shows that it has been under cultivation for many years, yet the soil is as fruitful as ever. The waters of the Rio Grande, like the waters of the Nile in old Egypt, carry the top soil of the mountains in which they have their source, and deposit it year after year upon the land, keeping it up to its full bearing power.

The grape-vines and gardens are generally surrounded by *adobe* walls connecting with the *adobe* houses of the inhabitants, and it is a singular sight to see a landscape where all there is has but one color. Everything is of the color of the soil. The *adobe* bricks of which the houses are built are made on the spot where the houses are to stand. A hole is dug, and the clay is mixed with water in the pit. The bricks are moulded in wooden moulds, and are generally eighteen inches long, ten to twelve wide, and four to five inches thick. In a week's time they are dried sufficiently to be put into walls. Some more of the soil is mixed with water, and this furnishes the cement to bind the structure together.

You see, Mother Nature has furnished everything ready at hand to build a house, except the timber for the roof, which is supplied from the luxuriant growth of cottonwood on the shores of the Rio Grande and the irrigating canals, and this is the only material that has to be brought from the water's edge.

Few of the houses in the suburbs of Juarez have glass windows. As a rule, a square hole in the wall with a tight wooden shutter, open all day, summer or winter, furnishes all the light needed in the house. The cooking, washing, and eating are all done out of doors. The houses I have had an opportunity to look into do not seem to be overstocked with furniture. A bedstead or two, and a bench, constituted all there was, and even these showed that the enterprising Yankee had been around and had sold the Mexicans "Grand Rapids" furniture.

I intended to take you to Juarez first, because there you can see all grades of houses and all classes of Mexican people, from the pure white Castilians (the military officers in the Presidio) to the black and tawny peons; houses furnished with all the luxury of Europe or America, and houses like those I have described above. You even find the gratings that separate the lovers in Spanish novels, and which project in front of the house to allow the señoritas a look up and down the street. In my next I will try to sketch the houses and streets, and fill them with the people by whom they are inhabited.

XV.

EL PASO, TEXAS, *April* 1, 1893.

YOUR letter of the twenty-third of March has pleased me very much. It showed that all honest efforts to instruct people are successful, provided the seed is planted in the proper soil. From the tenor of your letter I judge that I have made no mistake in the selection of my audience.

In my last I promised to take you over to Juarez again, and show you the houses and the streets filled with people. Well, it is mighty easy to make rash promises, but it is not nearly as easy to fulfil them.

During the last eight or ten days the temperature has increased to such an extent that all efforts to do anything become hardships. Think of it: our rooms in the hotel are up to seventy-five degrees Fahrenheit right along, and in the daytime the thermometer registers, with windows and doors open, a temperature of from seventy-eight degrees to ninety degrees. To go over to Juarez in such weather is asking altogether too much—even in imagination—and I will have to suspend our trip until a "norther" cools the atmosphere to some extent.

But of course there is no objection to taking a look at our hotel and its guests, especially as you will not have to travel a great way; and, on the whole, the heat here is not very oppressive, the air being so dry that you don't feel it much. The great trouble is to supply the inner man with moisture enough to counteract the rapid evaporation through the pores of the skin.

So, you see, the place where this moisture is supplied may properly form the starting point from which we will visit the Hotel Vendome. The bar-room is located on the corner of St. Louis Street, and the bar is presided over by Mr. Potter of Texas, assisted by a gentleman of the colored persuasion who does the rough work (cleaning the glasses, wiping off the counter, and so forth), while Mr. Potter dispenses the drinks with gentlemanly politeness.

I have studied the drinks carefully, and can recommend one of Mr. Potter's specialties. He brews a milk punch unsurpassed in my experience. Adjoining the bar-room proper is another room, which serves as a sort of sitting-room for those who want to have the time extended during which the cooling drinks pass the lips. In one corner of this room is a little closet or small room, partitioned off for those guests who enjoy a little private game of cards; and, between us, I must tell you that I myself had an invitation to a game of "round-up," which I had, however, to decline on account of my ignorance of it, and for some other reasons which will appear later on. From these rooms we pass to the reading-room, where the "drummers" do their writing, and where in the evening the "regulars" come together to tell stories.

When I speak of the "regulars" I mean those of the guests who have been here for some length of time, in a measure permanent boarders. Of

course, some go and others take their places, but nobody is admitted in less time than a week or two. Most of these "regulars" are "lungers," and they usually introduce themselves by a long description of all their ailments, and their experiences in the different sections of the country where they have been. This is not the most cheerful part of the introduction, but it generally don't last long, because there are other "regulars" who have already told their tales.

One of our coterie is a gentleman, formerly from Kingston, N. Y., who is a representative of the original Californian "Forty-niners." He landed there, I think he said, with the first lot by way of Panama. He was in

Nevada during the time when Mark Twain ran a store in Carson City, and he knows every man, woman, and child that ever lived on the Pacific Slope. The business he is on now is a "gold mine" that he discovered sixty miles from here, and he is looking for some one to buy it from him.

Then we have the "dominie," a Presbyterian preacher, who is here to regain his voice. He puts the company on their good behavior, and "cuss" words don't sound good when he is around. We have the "judge"; he is a lawyer, from Louisiana, I think, but he is an old resident here, and does a little private business in the little room referred to above. In fact, he gets acquainted with new-comers quicker than anybody else, and it often happens that he takes parties of three over to the bar, and, later on, a social game is played, and they say the "judge" usually wins.

Then we have the "gentleman from Kentucky"—or, I should say, we had, because he left us a week ago to go to Las Vegas. He was thoroughly posted on horses; but the knowledge that he possessed of all kinds of drinks proved him to be a true son of old "Kentuck." In addition to these we have the "gentleman from Michigan," who has travelled a good deal in Mexico. He can tell more about the effects of the Mexican national drink, *tuquela*, than about the scenery; and, besides these, we take in "transients" to fill out the gaps.

But I had almost overlooked the father of the "regulars." He is from Delaware; has been an engineer in "Uncle Sam's" service; has surveyed the Indian Territory, and tells Indian stories that confirm you in General Sherman's view, "that the only good Indian is a dead Indian." He is now a peach-planter in Delaware, where his father and his grandfather before him have lived, and he is here for the benefit of his health.

Then we have, every day, new faces. One day it is an English lord and his family; the next day it is a Scotch laird, who, with his daughter, takes long walks, and wears shoes with hob-nails. These honor us with a short stay.

And what do you think! John Wanamaker is expected here to-morrow! (Of course, it would be sinful to travel on Sunday.) He will stop over for the day, and our parson has told me that he will be invited to preside at a Sunday-school convention which is especially called on his account.

Our landlord is like all others I have met, and the "house" is as much like other country hotels as one egg is like another; so it is not worth while to waste any paper on either.

XVI.

EL PASO, TEXAS, *April* 2, 1893.

IN my last I referred to a gentleman who represents in our set of "regulars" the "pioneer" of the early days of California, and the glorious times when a private graveyard constituted an essential part of a gentleman's equipment in Nevada.

The incidental mention of this gentleman in connection with half a dozen or more of others would hardly do justice to a man whose life has been so varied, and who has seen so much of pioneer life in the far West. To give you an idea of the man, I will say he is six feet one in his stockings; his eyes are as keen as a knife-edge; he is broad-shouldered, and his fists would do honor to a prize-fighter. His weight would be somewhere near one hundred and ninety, and his hair and beard are of a gray color. He looks like a man who has seen a good deal of life, and who can take care of himself in any case.

Now you might expect that a man of this type would be overbearing and surly, but you were never more mistaken. He seems to be a jolly, overgrown boy, who likes to spin yarns by the hour, and is ever ready to relate the hair-breadth escapes he has had. I met him in front of the hotel a week or two ago, and he started a conversation.

I soon learned that he was an old Californian miner, that he had discovered a gold mine in New Mexico, and was looking for some capitalists to take an interest in his mine and work it. He next had to show me some of the ore, which he kept in the hotel yard. To demonstrate how rich it was, he pounded up a piece of rock about as big as his fist in an iron mortar, and then began to wash it out, in the same manner that he had washed out gold in California, when a panful of earth produced from sixty to five hundred dollars. This piece of rock would only show color; at least I thought I could see something yellow on the edge of the dirt in the pan after he had washed it out. I felt interested. I had never seen anybody wash out gold, and his stories of rich finds in California also interested me; so, as he seemed to take a liking to me, he in a short time became a member of the "regulars."

I tell you this simply to introduce our "pioneer" and give him an opportunity to tell some of the stories which have furnished no small part of our entertainment for some time. It would be impossible for me to give an outline of his tales. I will, therefore, tell them as nearly as possible in his own words; or, rather, let him tell them himself.

He got a-going on some of his Californian stories in this way. Some guests returned to the hotel one evening with a good string of ducks that they had shot on some pools of water not a great way from El Paso. After the game had been regularly inspected, the conversation turned on hunting. From ducks it went to jack-rabbits; from these to deer and antelope; finally, bears and mountain lions came up, and then our friend from California had a story to tell. "You see," he began, "when I first went to California, in '49, the mountains were full of grizzly bear. I had many a hard fight with them, and killed a great number; but there was one old fellow (he weighed fourteen hundred pounds) who gave us a great deal of

trouble. I went for him more than once, but, somehow or other, he always got away; so, finally, I concluded to trap him.

"I knew pretty near where his den was, and, to make sure of him, built a pen and baited it with a calf. Sure enough, he got in, and I had him alive. A live bear, of course, was a valuable animal in those days, and he was the making of me at that time. The first thing I did, I took him down to the settlement, and we had a bear-and-bull fight. I charged a dollar a head to see it, and I cleared sixty dollars. I then sold the bear for fifty dollars in gold, fifty dollars' worth of provisions, two jackasses, and a jenny. I loaded my asses with the groceries and started for the mines. I sold them for a greatly advanced price, and inside of three months I had no less than ten mule teams travelling between Sacramento and the mines, making money hand over fist, and all started from that one bear."

This story was received with general acclamation, and other story-tellers attempted to show off; but when the question of raising large vegetables came up, he started in to give another one.

"You know," he said, "that in the early days the Sacramento Valley was the most fruitful part of the whole State, and the vegetables and fruit raised there were simply grand. Talk about pumpkins in Connecticut—why, they were nowhere. There was a friend of mine who had a farm outside of the city. His name was Jack Hamilton, and he had originally come from New Hampshire. He raised pumpkins, and he showed me some that weighed over two hundred pounds apiece. Well, one day an old sow with a litter of pigs was missing. They looked all around for them, but could not find hair nor hide of her or the pigs. About a week after the sow had got lost, my friend wanted to take one of the pumpkins—of course, the largest one of the lot—to the county fair; when, lo and behold, they found that the old sow had eaten a hole into the pumpkin, and had lived for a week with her litter inside of it on the pumpkin seeds."

This was a corker. It settled the question as to the size of pumpkins on the Pacific Slope once and for all. No one could beat it, and our meeting adjourned then and there to the bar-room, where all of us took one as a reward of merit, and then separated to go to bed, which is precisely what I intend to do now.

So, good-night.

XVII.

El Paso, Texas, *April* 3, 1893.

I HAVE described to you our Plaza a number of times, I believe, and have in a general way given you a description of the people who usually sit around in it; but I will now go a little more into details.

In the centre of the Plaza is the fountain with its basin and its two alligators. Directly northwest of it is a pavilion intended for the band which, years ago, when the "boom" was on, played there daily. You may remember that one Sunday, some weeks ago, I had to close my letter to listen to a band of Mexican musicians who performed at that time. It was a string band of six pieces: two fiddles, a bass-viol, one harp, one clarionet, and a trumpet, and I tell you the music was not bad. The leader, a little hunchback not over four feet high, made his violin "talk," as my friend from Delaware remarked while we sat on a stone wall listening.

The Plaza was crowded with people. The visitors from the North and

East furnished a large quota, but the Mexicans outnumbered them. I saw few Mexican women, but close to my side was an old señora who was all attention. She was dressed in black, and had a shawl thrown over her head which completely covered her face, so that I could not even get a glimpse of it. I have no doubt, however, that she was in some way interested in one of the performers. Most of the Mexicans wore broad-brimmed hats. But few were dressed in the gorgeous style described to you in one of my former letters. Ragged clothes and dirty blankets were in the majority, and I noticed one among the lot who wore sandals instead of shoes, and they were rather the worse for wear.

The music was all new to me. Its soft strains seemed to invite you to have day-dreams and to conjure up long-forgotten events. I stayed there

listening for hours, and then went home filled with recollections of other times and other places. This was the only concert we had had, so far, on the Plaza, but I have listened to this same band again and again, and with the same pleasure.

You see, the proprietor of the "Tepee" has them engaged permanently to furnish music to his customers in the gambling-hall, where faro and keno are played; and all you have to do to enjoy divine music, is to go into the hall, sit down, and play or order drinks, and you are welcome. The house is always crowded, and the business at the bar and gaming-tables is flourishing.

But to return to my original theme; namely, to describe our Plaza on a warm, sunny day. I will have to introduce you to the people who sit around the music-stand. There, as in the Vendome, we have "regulars" and "transients," and, of course, the "regulars" of the hotel are recognized as old settlers.

The first figure I have to introduce is "our Frenchman." He has travelled all over Europe and has visited all the countries that border on the Mediterranean. He knows Algeria and Tunis as well as you and I know New York and Hoboken; and he can tell you all about the costumes of the people of Asia Minor, as well as of the people who promenade on the Boulevard Montmartre in Paris. When he starts in, every one is all attention. With the point of his cane he draws maps on the sand (or, as one of my friends put it, in the bacteria that cover the ground). He knows all the past and present of European politics, and lays down with absolute certainty the future of the European states. In American matters he is not as well posted; but we have an Irishman who knows all about that. While listening to *his* dissertations I have often thought of the old familiar saying, "that it was a pity that when the Lord made this world he did not have the advice of some of the wise men of the present day." What a paradise it would have been, could he have done so!

Then we have transients who have just come from the North, others from the East, and a good many from New Mexico; and the discussions about the laws and customs of the different sections and countries are endless. An amusing incident occurred the other day. A late arrival from Carson City, Nevada, began to tell of his experience in the "early days." Our friend, the Californian pioneer, interrupted him. "Why, I was sheriff of that county in 1860, and *I* am the man who impanelled the jury and subpoenaed the witnesses in that trial between Hyde and Morgan in the 'landslide case,' tried by ex-Governor Roop in Carson City." He related the story as if he had committed "Mark Twain's" description to memory. But he closed his tale with the remark that "Mark Twain" had him in his picture of the scene. After this evidence was in, there was nothing more to be said. I had always looked upon that court scene as one of the great author's finest efforts in inventional writing, and here in the "wild" West I find the man who, with one fell blow, destroys my fancy.

What do you think, however, when I tell you that there is a man in Mr. Clemens' picture of the court-room who actually bears a slight resemblance to our Californian friend! I know you would not be without a copy of "Roughing It," and I therefore refer you to page 244, where you will see, behind the judge's desk, a broad-shouldered gentleman with a high, soft-crowned hat—the sheriff who ran the court.

So it goes. All our illusions go to pieces sooner or later. Mark

Twain's "Roughing It" is removed from the field of romance to that of history; and I think, whenever you wish to instruct the pupils in our schools on the history of Nevada, you should adopt it as a text-book.

XVIII.

EL PASO, TEXAS, *April* 4, 1893.

I PROMISED to show you Juarez in holiday attire, and I now have an opportunity to do so. It is Easter Sunday, and, the temperature having kept low, we will take a buggy—that is, you and I, and Carl and his friend from England on their ponies will serve as guides.

As I told you before, there are two bridges connecting Juarez with El Paso, both owned by the International R. R. Co., and on both toll is collected. This time, however, we go over as dry-shod as the Jews did when Moses led them across the Red Sea, and it does not cost us a cent. During the past two or three weeks the Rio Grande has actually disappeared. With the exception of a dirty pool here and there, there is not a drop of water in its wide, sandy bed, and our enterprising Mexicans who had started the ferry are completely thrown out of business.

The bed of the river presents a desolate appearance. Sand, sand, and nothing but sand, and it looks impossible that it should ever be filled again. Yet on the Mexican as well as on the American shore men are at work raising and securing the levees, to guard against such freshets as have heretofore overflowed both banks and shifted the bed of the stream half a mile over toward Mexico.

We enter Juarez by the same street on which the horse-cars go in, and we notice at once that a great feast day is about to be celebrated. On all the prominent buildings, the custom-house, post-office, and presidio, as well as on many private buildings, the green, white, and red flag of the Republic is floating, and the houses and stores are decorated with bunting of the same colors. Over the office of the American consul floats the Stars and Stripes, and here and there smaller flags indicate that the residents of some of the houses are Americans.

The inhabitants are in motion to reach the Plaza, and you see them coming in from the country in wagon loads, or riding on horses and burros. In not a few cases a whole family is on a single horse, the woman, with a child in her arms, riding in front of her husband. A great many of the men are well dressed, but the everlasting black in the ladies' dresses becomes in time monotonous. As we pass on, nearing the Plaza, the crowd increases, and you now see here and there young women who have adopted the American costume, high-heeled shoes and high-colored dresses, but very few have any use for spring bonnets.

Opposite one corner of the Plaza is the establishment of Mr. Duchene, a Swiss who served years ago in the United States regular army, married a Mexican, and settled down as a wine-seller. Here we hitch our team and the ponies, and are now ready to view the town at our ease.

The Plaza is decorated with flags and bunting. Around the pedestal of the Juarez monument Mexican flags are draped in an artistic manner, and lamp-post, tree, and shrub are decorated.

We stroll along with the people who are promenading on the Plaza, and at last take a seat facing the old church. The Plaza is alive with strange figures. Señoritas in twos and threes pass by. Here and there are dark Indian faces alongside of pure white. The majority are dressed in black, with black shawls thrown over their heads, and rarely is a light dress or an American bonnet seen.

The men, dressed in their national costume—some in bright colors, others in rags—did not promenade with the señoritas, but supplied all the color there was in this sombre picture.

The service in the cathedral had taken place in the morning, so we had no opportunity to see it; but I must not forget a visit during service made on the previous Thursday.

The church was filled then from end to end with women wrapped in black shawls, but here and there an American dress, and even a bonnet, was seen. As we approached the door we saw that all were on their knees facing the altar, where eight or ten wax candles made the darkness more visible. As there were no men in the church, except those who like statues stood on the right and left of the altar, we soon withdrew and took seats on the Plaza, facing the church; and for an hour the people entered and left the sanctuary.

I had noticed on previous occasions that most of the Mexican women and girls were, on week days, of a very dark complexion, and was surprised that I should see so many much lighter faces on the Sundays I spent in Juarez; and I also seemed to notice a change in the looks of the señoritas on our side of the river.

Among the "regulars" I have mentioned my friend the peach-planter from Delaware. He is looked upon by all of us as the best judge of female beauty, having studied it in all sections of the country, and I submitted my difficulty to him. "Why," he said, "don't you know that the Mexican women of the lower classes wash themselves every Sunday and feast day?—so that the question resolves itself into a query as to the quality of the soap in most cases. But at times"—and he gave me a side glance of his eyes—"in addition to simply washing, I have no doubt *whitewashing* comes in also." Be that as it may, after drinking a bottle of Mr. Duchene's native Mexican wine, we started on to see more of the town and its surroundings.

The presidio is, next to the custom-house, the largest public building. Like all others, it is built in the form of a hollow square. It is a handsome brick structure, and serves as barracks, hospital, etc., of a regiment of Mexican soldiers. As we approached the entrance we saw, coming behind us, two whole companies in their gray summer costume, accompanied by two officers in full uniform. It seems that every Sunday these soldiers are given an outing, and to make sure that none of them run away, the first and second lieutenants have to go with them. The soldiers were unarmed, but each officer carried a revolver, as did the policemen and the custom-house officers we saw on the border of the Rio Grande.

We asked permission to go into the barracks; it was granted, and we thus had an opportunity to see the soldiers at home. The officers are white men, and in their looks and actions reminded me strongly of Frenchmen; and so did the soldiers, in a certain way. They were all of them broad-shouldered, healthy-looking fellows of medium height and of an exceedingly dark brown color.

Entering through the gateway, where two soldiers with Remington rifles stood on guard, we found ourselves in a square yard surrounded by buildings one story high, and a colonnade. On the right are the b a r r a c k s proper. A look in showed the knapsacks, canteens, and fire-arms systematically hung upon the wall, and the bedsteads of the soldiers, about two feet apart, extending along the room. When I say bedsteads I must give you some description of the piece of furniture meant. It is simply a low sort of table, six feet or so in length, with legs about six inches higher on the end next the wall than on the outer end. It is certainly simplicity itself, and it reminded me of the carpenter who took his nap during the dinner hour on the soft side of a plank.

Opposite this room, across the yard, is the hospital, in which, however, real beds are furnished for the sick. The side facing the entrance has another dormitory, which leads to a yard where the kitchen, and, I think, the lock-up, is located. This yard also contains the tanks that supply water to the garrison. Every drop of water has to be pumped by hand. A driven well at one end of the tanks is provided with a cast-iron Yankee pump, which is kept in operation by those of the soldiers who have broken some of the rules.

The whole place is as neat as a pin, and, all in all, is a credit to the officers and men who are quartered there.

From the presidio we go on through some of the best streets in the town, and also through others most singular-looking to a stranger. In one section, evidently of late construction, not one of the adobe houses is plastered or whitewashed. The streets, houses, and adobe walls that surround the yards are of one color. Everything you see is a dark gray, and it is difficult to distinguish at a short distance where the street ends and the houses begin. The main streets, however, have a cheerful look. All the houses are, at least on the street front, plastered and whitewashed; and some walls are even laid out in squares, to give the appearance of stone buildings. Here we saw the gratings on the windows referred to in a former letter.

On one occasion we saw two young ladies (they were almost white, and their beauty was only marred by a little too much mouth, as my friend from Delaware declared) looking through the bars and smiling at the passing "Gringoes," who returned their smiles with interest.

I suppose your Spanish is, like mine, of negative value, and I may as well tell you what "Gringo" means. It is a man who speaks only an incomprehensible language, and every stranger who does not speak Spanish is so called here; the same as my fellow-countrymen, during the "middle ages," called any one who could not speak the language of the "Fatherland" a "Welschmann."

After we left the city we came to the real agricultural wealth of the neighborhood. Every foot of the ground is cultivated. The whole country is intersected by irrigating canals, which are elevated above the surrounding farm land, and look like embankments, or, rather, raised roadways.

Grapes, corn, wheat, and all kinds of fruits are grown here to perfection. The farm-houses, *adobe* buildings in a hollow square, are scattered all over the country. What surprised me most was a discovery I made about pigeon-houses. Some time ago I looked through some books illustrating the Egypt of the present day. The villages of the peasantry, with their flat-roofed dwellings, were just like those of the Mexican peasantry.

In addition to this, the pigeon-houses were similar. Here are real pigeon-houses built of *adobe*, three, four, and five stories high, as they are on the Nile ; and it is pretty certain that at the time Moses lay in the bulrushes this was already an old style.

Our trip into the country brought us to another *adobe* church. It was not very old, but it had a most characteristic bell-tower. In front of the main entrance were two posts planted about ten feet apart, each forked on the upper end, and a pole resting in the forks completed the structure. Three bells were suspended by chains from the cross-beam at the height of about six feet from the ground. One of the bells bore the date of 1834 and the others 1854, showing that the church is of recent origin.

Well, I think with this last effort I will close my attempt to describe the city and people of Juarez. The more I write, the more firmly I become convinced that words are the poorest means of expressing thoughts.

What a blessing it would be if somebody would invent a machine to record the sights we see and the impressions they make on our minds. All would be easy then, for we could simply set the recorder in motion and show things much better than by clumsy words.

XIX.

EL PASO, TEXAS, *April* 6, 1893.

IN my last I closed my studies of the Mexicans, and will now take a look at the other fellows. To begin with, you will certainly expect me to start at the head. You and I have no doubt in our minds that the schoolmaster and his superior officer, the trustee, are at the head, and so we will start in by taking this proposition for granted.

I had taken a look at the high-school, the grammar-school, and some primary classes, some time ago; but, owing to the attraction of the other pole (metaphysically speaking), I then suspended operations, and did not take up that subject again until I felt that I had mastered the other. I met the superintendent just as he was mounting his horse to go to the negro school, which, under the State laws of Texas, is an independent institution. No white children can go to it, and no negro can attend a white school; and yet I saw children in the negro school *whiter than you or I.*

The superintendent is a man of fifty-five or fifty-six years of age. He

wears gold spectacles, and, being an Ohio man, is full of dignity. He regretted that his horse could not carry both of us, but kindly directed me to the negro school-house, where he met me at the door.

This school-house is a fine-looking new brick building, with two pleasant school-rooms in which eighty or ninety pupils are instructed. The principal is nearly white, and is assisted by a lady teacher of about the same color. Both hail from Rochester, N. Y., and when I was introduced as "Professor" Eickemeyer (in spite of my protest and statement that I was a "greasy mechanic"), both seemed to look upon me as a fellow-countryman.

Well, I was invited to the only chair in the class-room, which I gratefully accepted on the plea of being an invalid (which was, as Carl puts it, a bluff), and the teacher, or professor, as the judge called him, began to show us what his pupils could do. I noticed that all of them, from the primary to the seventh-year grade, were provided with books more or less the worse for wear; and I saw none of the appliances that are used in the primary grades of our schools, and in the primary classes for white children in El Paso. He called out the sixth-year boys and girls, six in number, and as they stood in a row I had a fair opportunity to look them over. On the extreme left was a tall boy, as black as the ace of spades; next to him was another, two or three shades lighter, while the next one would have passed anywhere as a white boy. The girls differed in size and color as much as the boys; one of them had blue eyes and flaxen hair. The exercises consisted of a spelling-bee, such as you can find, or could find a few years ago, in the schools of the city of New York. The words were read by the professor from a text-book which the pupils had studied just before they got up, and were of such a character that I felt sure not one of them knew their definitions; and I know, had I been put in the row, I would have got to the foot before the lesson was over. It reminded me of the old days when I saw the pupils change places when the one above missed.

He next called out another grade, and the same performance was repeated with slight variations.

I was then introduced to the pupils as "Professor" Eickemeyer, and was requested to address them. I did so, but did not repeat the same speech that Judge E———s had heard so many times that he finally thought it was his own. Of course, I complimented them on their acquirements, and did no less for the superintendent and teachers; and I think that Yonkers ought to be proud to be represented in El Paso by the most eloquent member of its school-board.

The next performance was singing, and this was really as good as you could expect. The song, the national air or anthem of Mexico, was new to me, and there were some very good voices. Then four girls sang a song, and the whole school (all the pupils had been brought into one room) sang the chorus. After the singing, which I applauded heartily, to the great enjoyment of the boys and girls, the superintendent, at the request of the "professor," delivered an address. He evidently fired at me, because I think his gun was elevated so high at the muzzle that the spryest young darky could hardly jump high enough to get in range. He talked for at least half an hour, and as I had to stand up in honor of the occasion, I felt about tired out; but in acknowledgment of the treat I had to sail in again and express my thanks. I am invited to meet the judge at the Spanish school next, and will report in due time what I see, hear, and, least and last, what I say myself.

P.S.—You see, the judge talked as if every little darky intended to be elected President of the United States at some future time.

XX.

El Paso, Texas, *April* 9, 1893.

I HAVE now spent over two months in El Paso, and have, in a measure, familiarized myself with it and its surroundings.

When I came here the Rio Grande contained at least some water, but all has now disappeared; and even the irrigating canals are nearly empty, although fed by a reservoir located some miles above. The rainfall here is insignificant, as any one would expect when they consider that the humidity is almost *nil*. To prevent evaporation, or at least to reduce it to a minimum, the canals are made narrow and deep, and even the ditches in the fields are dug deep and narrow, to present as little surface to the dry air as possible.

When trees or shrubs are to be irrigated, deep trenches, or rather pits, are made around them, and these are filled with water. Even when the grass-plot is to be watered it is not sprinkled as in our neighborhood; the water is run on in a heavy stream, which is absorbed by the loose soil as fast as it comes.

Land that has no water-supply is almost worthless; but whenever water is supplied, either artificially or by nature, it produces all the fruits of the temperate and semi-tropical zones. The first requirement for starting or running a cattle or horse ranch is water. Stock will not, I am told, stray more than twenty miles from the spring or brook which furnishes their supply, so that the cow-boy, or, as he is called here, the cow-puncher, is sure that he has gathered in or rounded up all the cattle on a given range when he has described a circle with a radius of twenty miles around his spring, gradually reducing the diameter until his herd is safely collected in the corral.

But it is of equal importance to the cow-boy to have a supply of fluid to irrigate the inner man, and this has started me on a train of thought which, I think, deserves to be followed. Up to the present time I have not had the pleasure of studying the "ranchmen," except as I saw them here in the "corral," when they came in for supplies. I always noticed that when they arrived, and the horses and mules had been taken care of, the first thing they did was to irrigate. I have described at length the various institutions where supplies of the nature in question are furnished, and it was an interesting problem to me what fluid these hardy men would select to quench their thirst. One would have thought that men who had just travelled thirty-five or more miles over a desert plain, would fall to and drink water by the pailful; but no, nothing of the kind. Water is the last thing they seem to hanker after. A stiff glass of some kind of fire-water is always sent ahead, and a few drops of water are used to wash it down afterward, more as a preparation, I think, to clear the passage for the next drink than to relieve the thirst.

Then, again, I have observed that when the ranchman returns he always carries some demijohns as a supply for himself, but never any water that I could see. That a visit to El Paso is an important event you may be sure. It is never undertaken unless supplies are needed badly. On all ranches they always have fresh meat on hand, and on many even fresh eggs; also Mexican beans—I think they call them *frijoles*—which grow almost everywhere. Taking all this into account, I reached the conclusion that the refilling of the demijohns is the principal object of the trip. I am strengthened in this opinion by another observation. To quench their thirst when they arrive here usually takes some days, showing conclusively that a drought had preceded their coming; and I know of a case when the return trip to the range was delayed for two days, to allow the company to pull itself together.

But let us go a little farther into this interesting question. That a ranchman, whose drinking-water is always more or less alkaline in its nature, should want to put a stick in it, does not seem on the whole very strange; but how can we account for the methods of irrigation of people who have no such adverse circumstances to contend with? No wonder that man and beast have to irrigate in a climate like this of Western Texas; but how can we account for the phenomenon in countries where the hygrometer shows ninety to one hundred degrees of humidity? I feel that I made a great mistake that I did not come here years ago.

Suppose the irrigation problem, as far as the human species is concerned, was regulated or influenced by general humidity. What valuable conclusions could I not have drawn during my life, and especially during my travels, where I had ample opportunities to study the drinks of almost all nations! Think of it: if I had taken as a starting point all the mixtures in use in this climate, where humidity is *nil*, and, while watching the humidity of other lands, studied their drinks, I might have solved the question why the Englishman takes his Scotch whiskey with soda, while the Scotchman takes it straight; why the South-German takes his morning drink in the beer-house and winds up late at night with a bottle of wine and a cup of black coffee, while to the North-German a glass of schnapps serves as his morning drink and his night-cap.

Then, again, it might solve the problem why Medford rum holds its own in New England, while Blue Grass whiskey is marching victoriously through the Middle States. You see, the problem is a great one; but, alas! I am not in it. I began at the wrong end. Yet I am sure that the suggestion is a good one, and if some clear-headed thinker would take it up properly, he could solve one of the greatest sociological questions for the benefit of humanity.

XXI.

EL PASO, TEXAS, *April* 10, 1893.

I HAVE just learned something, and as I have a few minutes and nothing particular to do (being, as it were, between drinks), I will have to tell it to you while it is fresh in my mind. Here, as all over the States south of Mason and Dixon's line, we have two kinds of Grand Army posts, the "Gray" and the "Blue." There has been a great deal said about shaking hands over the bloody chasm; and the incident I have to relate will show you that there is a good deal of fiction in some of these stories. But, to get to my tale.

Both Grand Army posts have their "camp-fires," as they call them; that is, they light their pipes, sit around and tell stories, and, as I am informed, irrigate, to enliven the company.

It so happened that the two posts lighted their camp-fires on the same evening last week. The "blues" were peacefully sitting around, telling stories of Sheridan's ride, and other equally well-authenticated stories of the civil war, when, lo and behold, a squad of rebels appeared at the door, took the doorkeeper or sentry prisoner, conquered the assembled braves, and marched every man of them as prisoners to the Confederate headquarters.

Here a court-martial was formed, and the poor, helpless captives were condemned to smoke Confederate tobacco out of corn-cob pipes, to drink Confederate whiskey, and to eat Confederate beans (not the mild kind so well known as "Boston baked beans," but that horrid species known around here as the Mexican black bean, or *frijole*, seasoned with red pepper to such an extent that the poor victim has to keep drinking in sheer self-defence). The "rebels" kept their prisoners till the small hours of the morning, and then dismissed them, singing "Dixie." You may imagine how our brave boys in blue felt under this treatment. They were outraged, and I have learned from good authority that they have sworn to take revenge on the "rebel" crew.

All the "blues" in the State, or rather county, are to be called in at the next camp-fire, to make sure that no "rebel" will escape. But, I beg of you, don't tell anybody of this part of the conspiracy, because the "rebels" might hear of it and get scared and decamp.

The proposition is to retaliate in kind, and go them one better. A resolution was passed unanimously, that no "rebel" should escape "till daylight does appear."

Now talk about relegating the "bloody shirt" to the relics of the past. You see the "rebels" flaunt it still in the faces of the Union men, and it looks to me as if the "Sons of the Veterans," even, will be in honor bound to act as their fathers do in the sunny South.

P.S.—I forgot to mention that the boys propose to sing "John Brown's body lies a-mouldering in the grave."

XXII.

EL PASO, TEXAS, *April* 10, 1893.

THE last week or two I devoted to a study of the other El Paso, and I find that there is hardly anything to mention. Of the churches I can say that they are like those at home—services twice every Sunday, and Sunday-schools in all of them. Even the church sociables are on the same general plan, as I have learned from my friend the "parson," who attended no less than three last week, in all of which ice-cream and cake were served at the close. So you see I may as well make my studies when I get home, and compete for the gold prizes offered by the *Statesman* to encourage home literature and improvement. And I now feel well posted in such studies. I could start in with the Italians behind my house, and study the manner of living of the Lazaroni of Naples and Southern Italy. Then I could step over to the Greek-Catholic church and learn all about the habits and customs of the inhabitants of the Danubian states. The old Teutonia Hall would furnish any number of pictures of the Hebrews who have been driven out of Russia and Poland by the Czar. And the new Teutonia Hall would supply the modern Teuton in all his glory. If I then took the health officer as my mentor and guide, and travelled with him once more, as I have many times before, I would have a field for my studies as varied as that I find here.

The great trouble, however, would be that I would have to put on green spectacles so as not to see all the things I could see and describe. As I intend to stay in Yonkers for some time to come, my pen-pictures might get me into trouble. So, come to think of it, I will confine my literary efforts to subjects away from home and not try to win the "gold prize."

To-morrow there is an election here for city officers—mayor and aldermen—and if you read the editorials of the El Paso "dailies," and compared them with those I read a week or so ago in the Yonkers papers, they are as like each other as two peas. One candidate represents a ring; the other wants the office for personal reasons. But what amused me most was that one of the candidates who was nominated withdrew because his employers objected to his running. Well, our Yonkers boy had spunk enough to run, and I glory in it and am glad of his success.

Then there is the water-supply question, which is, of course, a very important one; and the discussions you hear about it remind me of Yonkers twenty years ago, when some of our "best" citizens (*Statesman*) held indignation meetings, and some of my friends covered themselves with glory by shaking bottles filled with dirty water in the faces of those stupid water commissioners who, after three years' investigation, did not know as much as the gentlemen who had simply looked at the problem from *their* high scientific standpoint.

It cost the city of Yonkers a good many thousand dollars to convince our "best citizens" that they knew nothing, and I fear El Paso will also have to pay a nice penny before the wise men will learn the same lesson. So you see, even in this line I have nothing to write, because you can read the whole of it in the *Statesman* and *Gazette* of twenty years ago. And there you can find all the points fully elaborated, signed, sealed, and delivered by the heroes themselves.

But I must not forget a monument that is the glory of Mesa Garden. Fifteen years or so ago, by a lucky accident some genius discovered in Cardiff, N. Y., the well-known Cardiff giant. It was the wonder of the day; all the papers were full of it, and the illustrated papers contained large wood-cuts. A heated discussion was carried on as to its origin; but it was finally decided to be of that class of bug that Professor Agassiz classed as humbug.

Imagine my surprise and pleasure when I found myself face to face with this celebrated "giant." It seems that when its usefulness as a catch-penny had departed, an enterprising showman loaded it on a car to send it by way of El Paso to Mexico, to fleece the "Greasers." He was unfortunate, however. While trans-shipping it from one car to another, the baggage smashers handled the box in the same way they handle Saratoga trunks, and the result was bad. Both legs of the "giant" were broken, and the skeleton appeared in plain sight. Two bars of iron an inch square had formed the thigh and shin bones; this at once destroyed its use as an ossified man. After some time, the railroad company presented the mutilated relic to the owner of the Mesa Garden, where the "giant" now rests in peace.

Some other things differ slightly from what we are in the habit of seeing at home. El Paso County has an excellent court-house. It is erected in the centre of a square, with galleries on all sides, square towers on the corners, and a central tower, with a flight of stairs to the top, lighted by circular openings, and surrounded by handsome railings which extend to the top floor, forming a dome-shaped centre in the building. The court-house has four entrances, and, what is most appropriate, over each entrance is a Goddess of Justice, blindfolded and holding a balance, indicating that at least four kinds of justice are administered in the edifice.

The court-rooms, and those of the county officers, are comfortable and well lighted, and, what is more, they are all well furnished. Some time ago I visited this court-house to take a view of the city from the tower, and, as the court was in session, I took a seat and listened to the proceedings.

It was a jury trial, and the case had some novel features. It seems that a Mr. Roe had deposited in a certain bank five hundred dollars, and had taken a cashier's check for the amount. Some time later he stopped payment. The check was presented at another bank, properly indorsed by one of the owners of a gambling establishment, and it was cashed. When presented later to the first bank, payment was refused, and suit was brought to compel payment. The case was decided in favor of the plaintiff, on the ground of *innocent holder*.

The proceedings were carried on in the usual way, but all the lawyers and the jurymen in the box smoked pipes and cigars. The judge, the witness on the stand, and the lawyer who had the witness in hand were the only persons inside of the railing who did not smoke. Well, different countries, different fashions. So it goes.

Three weeks ago our Plaza was as gray as all the country around; but about that time the work to put it in shape began, and the first thing done was to clean the grass-plots of the sand and dust that the winter winds had deposited. A number of industrious Mexicans went to work with brooms to sweep the grass, in the same manner that our good housewives sweep the carpets. After considerable effort the blades of grass came to the surface. Water was then put on in streams, and to-day the grass is as green as on a well-kept lawn. The trees are in leaf, and the rose-bushes that surround the basin are in full bloom. The change was so rapid that it seemed as if you could see the grass grow.

Birds are very rare. In fact, I have seen none except a kind of red-breasted sparrow—the Mexican sparrow, I am told; but even these are few and far between. I wonder why some of the people up North who hate the English sparrow so much, don't catch them and send them down here where they would be welcome.

I have one more important person to mention, and then I will close to my satisfaction, and, I have no doubt, to yours. You have probably heard of the representative from Texas at the Republican nominating convention a year ago, who, when asked about offices, remarked : " What are we here for if not for the offices ? " This gentleman of national fame is a resident of El Paso. He is in charge of Uncle Sam's custom-house, and I saw him at the time I lost that half-dollar at the cock-fight in Juarez.

P.S.—The Democratic papers here call him, "What-are-we-here-for F——n."

XXIII.

EL PASO, TEXAS, *April* 11, 1893.

I LANDED here in El Paso on the first of February last, and the first time I got beyond the Plaza in front of the hotel was on the twenty-second of that month.

Besides the Plaza, El Paso has a park about two miles from the centre of the city. It was formerly owned by the El Paso Jockey Club, which flourished during the "boom"—up to 1888. When the "boom" subsided the Jockey Club did the same, and the city purchased the property for use as a public park.

Texas, like all other States, has its Arbor Day, and the governor selected as the Arbor Day for 1893, the twenty-second of February. The selection of Washington's Birthday was a happy one. The aldermen provided two hundred young trees to be planted. The McGinty Band was engaged to furnish the music, and, after a prayer by one of the leading clergymen, a patriotic speech was made by one of the leading lawyers, and the whole audience then adjourned to see the trees planted in holes already prepared by some Mexican laborers.

As stated above, the park is two miles or thereabouts from the centre of the town, and a few hundred feet from the tracks of the Southern Pacific Railroad. The manager of the road put two trains of five cars each at the disposal of the aldermen, and gave all those who wished to go a free ride to and from the park. This liberality was highly appreciated by the people of the city and the visitors. It looked as if all the churches, the schools, and the Sunday-schools were going on a picnic, and the crowd looked and acted exactly as a crowd would gathered up at home.

Few Mexicans were among the excursionists, although fully one-third of the inhabitants are of that nationality. The trains stopped near the gate of the park, and the visitors soon filled the grand stand. But the visitors by rail were not the only ones. Dozens of carriages and buggies brought ladies and gentlemen. But the small boy on the "burro" (donkey) cut the chief figure on the race-course. Everybody here rides on horseback, and a good many young men in Mexican saddles paraded about, at times starting around the track on impromptu races. But in spite of that the small boy had it all to himself. Most of the wood used is brought into town on burros, and these animals are more numerous than goats on Hog Hill. The only bridle used by the boys was an old rope wound around the burro's nose; and as to the saddle, why that is unknown in burro riding by boys. It was a lively picture when the cavalcade began to come in. Some youngster would ride, sitting as close to the head of the animal as he could,

while the next one preferred a seat near the tail; and other burros came in having two and even three riders on board. Now, a burro at times has his own views in regard to the direction in and the speed at which he wants to go, and as these may differ from those of the rider, a contest is often the result. It is highly amusing to see the amount of exercise he can furnish the small boy. To keep his animal in motion the boy has to use all the energy stored in his hands and heels, and even then the burro often goes his own way, after gracefully shooting his rider over his head.

When the whole audience had arrived and all were comfortably seated, the exercises began with music by the band, followed by prayer; then came the oration. I listened with a great deal of interest to the speech, which was patriotic and thoroughly American; yet I must own to some surprise when the speaker, in the course of his remarks, told his hearers that our free institutions had been brought over by the Pilgrim Fathers, had been maintained by the Fathers of the Republic, and that it was the duty of the children to preserve our freedom and deliver it to the future generation. I had not expected that an orator in Texas in 1893 would claim the Pilgrim Fathers as the founders of our free institutions. Yet it was not, after all, more of a surprise than the one I had in 1886, when a member of the English Parliament showed me over the Houses of Parliament in London. After we had visited the House of Commons—or, more properly speaking, the hall in which the sittings take place (as the House was not in session)—and while going to the House of Lords, we passed through a long hall, decorated on both sides with fresco paintings representing events in English history, one of which represented the embarkation of the Pilgrim Fathers on the *Mayflower.*

My friend had called my attention to the picture, and when I saw it the thought came into my mind that it would not take many more generations before the English would claim George Washington as one of the greatest Englishmen that ever lived; and my conductor, with a smile, assented to my suggestion.

The planting of the trees took quite some time, but a jack-rabbit furnished diversion for the small boy and the dogs. The poor fellow had been surprised near the grand-stand, and began to make his way in big leaps toward the fence. A whole drove of youngsters with a dozen or more of dogs took up the chase; but, fortunately for the rabbit, the fence was not rabbit-tight, though it was an effectual barrier for boys and dogs, so the rabbit escaped, thoroughly scared, no doubt.

The return train came in sight at about sunset, and all got safely home, having enjoyed a summer day on the twenty-second of February.

The Stars and Stripes waved over all public and many private buildings, and there was nothing to suggest that twenty-five short years ago the Texas Rangers stood in the line of the Confederates, fighting under Lee in defense of Richmond.

XXIV.

El Paso, Texas, *April* 11, 1893.

THE reason why I have been so very industrious lately in writing letters about El Paso is that El Paso has, among other things, some climate after all. About a week ago a season of blow set in, which, with more or less force, shifted the sands of the prairie all over the city. At times, especially on Thursday last, the wind blew a perfect gale of forty miles an hour for five hours, as I learned from the weather clerk, whose roost is almost opposite the hotel. The wind-gauge, a sort of whirligig, is a very interesting sight, and I have watched it with a great deal of attention. It can serve as a thermometer as well. When the breeze is light and the direction is east, the temperature is low and from sixty-five to seventy-five degrees in the shade; when from the west, the temperature rises from seventy-five or eighty degrees to ninety degrees or over. Now, the gale we have had came from the west, and the air being filled with dust and sand, I think I have a good conception of what a simoom in the Sahara may be like. The temperature of the moving air was above eighty degrees, and filled with sand and dust so that I could hardly see across the street, and it felt when I opened the window as if it came from a hot oven. The Plaza was deserted for two or three days; but the wind generally subsided when the sun went down, so that the evenings and nights were cool and pleasant. But you must not forget that when the temperature gets below seventy degrees in this dry atmosphere it is as cool as it is in Yonkers at sixty degrees, or even less.

Then, my stay here is drawing to a close, and I want to get over my self-imposed task. I hold you, however, responsible for all these letters. Your remark about the scarcity of water here started the whole of it, and after a while I began to like the task, and I think writing these letters to you has been as good a cure for my mind as the air has been for my body. I had to look sharp to be able to describe things, and then these studies put everything else out of my head, giving me, as it were, a vacation from all other thoughts and worries.

Next week I shall be in Santa Fé. But I doubt whether I shall continue in this line. You know that Mr. Deming, my nephew, has an atelier there and paints pictures; and I am strongly inclined to exchange the pen for the brush, and bring home such a work of art in landscape painting as no one has ever seen, or wanted to see!

I may send you a report on the election, which takes place to-day, if it continues to be windy, but, otherwise, I think the present letter will close the "Mysteries of El Paso."

XXV.

EL PASO, TEXAS, *April* 12, 1893.

WELL, the whirligig on the weather clerk's roost rotates at a good speed and the winds blow as before, but not anything like the whirlwinds that excited the legal and illegal voters of El Paso yesterday.

In El Paso, as elsewhere in this glorious country, the "best citizens" (as the *Statesman* usually calls them) at times take it into their heads to come to the front. You are sure to know them when you see them. All the year round they find fault with what others do. They never take any interest in public affairs except to find fault and to scold, and they feel rather above the common herd who vote and take an interest in the management of the city business. These gentlemen, with a flourish of trumpets, got up a citizens and taxpayers' party, held public meetings in the courthouse (which is used here for all sorts of entertainments, as well as for political meetings), and nominated a citizens' ticket. The Republicans, who are in the minority, did not make any nominations, but did not indorse the citizens' ticket either.

Yesterday the battle was fought. It was a bad day; the sand filled the air from morning till the polls closed, furnishing a good excuse for the "best citizens" to stay at home, and the result was as usual in such cases. The "straights" carried the election by a majority of over five hundred out of a vote of a little more than sixteen hundred, and the ticket, composed of pirates and blacklegs (as the "best citizens" assured the voters they were), was successful.

In this neighborhood the Mexicans are the unknown quantity. Out of sixteen hundred voters, about five hundred are Mexicans, and, of course, these were all bought by the "straights." The "best citizens" were altogether too good to do anything to get any Mexican votes, and even the few negroes were inveigled into voting the straight Democratic ticket. So it goes; but as virtue is said to be its own reward, I hope the "best citizens" feel entirely satisfied with the result.

Unbiassed observers told me before the election that both tickets contained the names of representative citizens, and that both candidates for mayor would make excellent officers.

I have, however, one more observation to make; namely, that not a solitary rum-shop keeper was on either ticket, and none has ever been elected as a city official in this place. The bar-rooms were absolutely closed, and, as the daily paper says, not even the river furnished an opportunity to irrigate.

In spite of these precautions, they had a lively time in what is called the "bloody Second." Two officers, a "regular" and a "special," got into an argument about a Mexican who was to be voted for one of the tickets, and both being well armed—the "special" with two six-shooters and a bowie knife, and the "regular" with one six-shooter and a "quoit" (a whip loaded with shot)—guns were drawn; but mutual friends (who seem to play an important figure in such affairs) separated them before a great deal of damage was done. Two bloody heads and some black eyes were the only results, and the report says that both officers attended to their duties at the same poll in the court-house as before. Other arguments and explanations took place at other polls, but as no damage was done, except to eyes and noses, they are not worth mentioning.

When the result was declared, the "unterrified" organized a procession to serenade the new mayor. A band was secured, and under the lead of my friend (the grand marshal who had conducted the St. Patrick's Day parade) they marched to the mayor-elect's residence, and after listening to a neat little speech of thanks and congratulation, adjourned to the "White House" to wind up the glorious victory.

If you look at the whole performance impartially, and make allowances for the difference in latitude between the two places, you will perceive that the dissimilarity is not as great between here and at home as you would expect when you consider that the two places are about two thousand miles apart; and it furnishes a new proof of the solidarity and unity of our free and glorious country.

P.S.—I forgot to relate a new use to which shooting-irons are put in this town. A week or two ago, in the evening, as I was just getting ready to retire, I heard a regular fusillade. Half a dozen shots were fired not a great distance from the hotel. A minute or two later the fire bells began to ring, and I was sure then that some cow-boys had taken the town and were murdering the inhabitants. I was mistaken, however; the shooting-irons served simply as a fire-alarm box to notify the firemen of a conflagration in a grocery store in San Antonio Street.

XXVI.

EL PASO, TEXAS, *April* 13, 1893.

MY son Carl has just returned from an excursion to a cattle ranch at Hueco Tanks, and his looks show, as well as the whirligig on the Weather Bureau, that the wind blows a gale. His eyes, his ears, and, he says, his lungs also, are filled with sand, and his clothing looks as gray as an *adobe* house.

You may remember that some time ago I introduced you to the owner of the corral known as the "Horse Restaurant," and to two ranchmen that we found there. Carl kept his saddle and obtained the horses used for his equestrian excursions at this place, and in a short time became acquainted with many of the cow-boys who frequented it. He accepted an invitation to visit Hueco Tanks with them, and the condition he was in when he returned, after a week's stay, was as stated above.

As luck would have it, he had a high wind going out and a gale coming back, but was well pleased with his experience. The owner of the ranch, described before as the "young man in Mexican costume" that we met at the corral, has a nice residence in El Paso, and is considered to be well-off. It was in company with him and two cow-boys that the excursion was made.

If Carl's description of the cattle ranch is at all correct, it must be a picturesque place.

But I can do no better than to give Carl an opportunity to tell his own story of the trip referred to above, as he did in a letter to a friend at home.

XXVII.

El Paso, Texas, *April* 14, 1893.

Dear Jack:

I have spent a good deal of time with the cow-boys down in this section, taking trips out to their ranches and into the mountains with them, and have gotten a fair insight into the cattle business.

There are only a few losses that the ranchman here has to guard against. He does not have to worry about cattle being frozen, taken sick, or straying very far from the "cow-camp," which is generally situated near the tanks or springs where they come to get water.

The ranches are not nearer to each other than fifty or sixty miles, and cattle will not stray more than twenty miles from water, unless the buffalo grass becomes moistened by rain or dew, and that is something that seldom happens. When it does, the grass dries very rapidly.

The ranges here are good and not overstocked. Occasionally a mountain lion will kill a calf or a yearling and eat from the flank until he is satisfied; then the wildcats will start in at the shoulder, while the coyote, who has been lingering about, keeping his eye on the feast, will pick at the carcass.

Now and then a cattle thief will start at the northern part of the State with a few head of cattle, and pick up others from the different ranches all along the way to the Rio Grande, where he will cross with them into Mexico. In this way they sometimes collect a herd of many hundred cattle, which they sell to the Mexicans. At other times the thieves are killed by some of the cow-boys before they reach their destination.

I have just come in from a visit to the ranch, and I must write you about the trip going out. The morning we started on our trip over the prairie, Tom and Jim came down to the corral at ten o'clock, and we three went up town to get some provisions, including canned corn, tanglefoot, etc. We got back at eleven and saddled the mustangs.

There was a horse for us to take out to the ranch for a rest. He had been pretty well worked out, but was just what we wanted for a pack-horse. I towed him out of the corral, and before going very far found that he would lead about as well as a wooden post.

We went down the turnpike about a mile to where Mrs. L. lives, and there Tom changed his clothes and got out the bedding we were to take along, besides some camping utensils, blankets, and a wagon cover. (Don't get this mixed up with the "tenderfoot's" cover for keeping the dust off wagons.)

The extra horse was then packed as usual, by first laying the wagon cover over him unfolded; on top of this came the blankets; next, two old oat-bags, tied together at the top, were laid across the horse, one hanging down on either side; they contained our cooking utensils and provisions. The wagon cover was then folded over the other things, and the whole tied tight around the horse with a lariat.

After this was done we started out, taking turns in leading the pack-horse. The wind was coming up at a great rate from the southwest, but as we were travelling with it we did not mind it so very much.

While I led the pack-horse by a rope around his neck, with a half-hitch around his jaw, the boys rode behind and kept him up with an occasional jab from a gun-stock or a kick in the ribs. This sort of work made my pony very nervous, as he was not yet four years old and only half broken. When we got to the first Mexican dug-outs, three miles from town, he tried to get away, but I was determined he should lead the other horse if it took a leg.

About two hundred yards from the dug-outs we saw two Mexicans driving a bunch of cattle off of the road on which we were travelling, and on nearing them Jim said : "There is a flying 'X' in that bunch." Tom told him to follow them and go through the bunch, and if he saw any to come back, and we would all go down and cut them out. But he did not find any of our cattle among them.

We started again, reaching the Mesa, when the pack-horse jerked back and pulled me clear of the stirrups. Just then the rope broke, and my pony started to run and buck—over mounds, cactus, mesquite, and sage bushes, and running around dagger plants, fortunately not leaving me on top of any of them. He kept this up for a quarter of a mile before he had his fill of the spurs with which I jabbed him at every jump. We both had a good sweat during the circus.

The boys had already started for the pack-horse, which had left as soon as the rope broke. When I came up, Tom handed me my six-shooter, which had been thrown out of the holster while the pony was bucking. It is a safe rule never to take your eyes off of a bronco's head ; if you do, he may have his feet on yours.

We tried to drive the pack-horse then, but he did not have the brains of a chicken, and would not keep road or trail ; and we found we were wearing our horses out trying to keep him in the right direction, so we finally concluded leading was the best.

The wind now was high, and picking up the dust and sand so that we could not see fifty feet in front of us, and we struck off for B.'s ranch, thinking we might find it, which we did, by good luck. It seemed as though his whole place was going to be covered up with the sand, that was drifting like so much snow.

His house was very comfortable and plain, being built of rough pine boards, but the cracks allowed considerable sand to blow in. On his place, which was fenced in, was a wind-mill for pumping water out of an artesian well into a large tank that was on high supports like a railroad tank. The mill was just humming on account of the high wind.

He had twelve dogs on the place, and they looked like thoroughbred meat-hounds, although he did not have their pedigrees. We had some coffee, eggs, and *frijoles* in the kitchen ; and after watering the horses and filling our canteens, we started on.

We could hardly tell what direction to start in, the air was so full of sand. Every trail was covered up, and there were no traces of a road, so we went it blind. Everything looked a yellowish cast from the sun shining through the sand-filled air, and we could just make out our shadows on the ground, which gave us our only idea of direction.

Each breath helped to fill our throats with the pure prairie sand, and we were entirely covered with it. The wind was so warm that it seemed like a hot blast. We kept pegging along over the rough road, our ponies in a trot all the way, occasionally sinking in up to their ankles when they would strike a gopher burrow.

At six-thirty or thereabouts the sun went down and the wind partially died out, and there in front of us, in the distance, stood Sierra Alto, which is the highest mountain of the Hueco chain, and stands fifteen miles east of

our camp. A peculiar thing about these rock mountains is that they are entirely bare of trees, but have a greenish hue from the mesquite and sage bushes, amolé, and Spanish dagger.

Finding we had struck three miles north of the main gap leading to the tanks, we went straight on over the first range of hills, and got on the northwest trail at dark. The dagger plants were all in bloom in this section of the country, and the cacti, with their beautiful red flowers, were in all directions more plentiful than near El Paso.

The short cucumber cacti had their tops covered with bright red flowers. The amolé or soap weed is of a dark green color. It grows low on the ground, and spreads like a century plant. From the centre, a distance of seven or eight feet, there shoots out a stalk of white, fibrous material, and on the top of this blossoms out a large bunch of white, bell-shaped flowers. The amolé is a tough plant on horses, as the thorns on the ends of the leaves break off in the hock joints when you do any fast riding over a country covered with them, where there is neither road nor trail, and if the thorns are not taken out at night the pony will not be fit to ride the next morning.

The Spanish dagger grows to the height of five or six feet, with a bunch of sharp leaves on the top, the lower ones having dried and fallen from the sides of a trunk which is sometimes six or eight inches in diameter. It is a

mean plant to ride against, as it will cut a hole in a leather boot as easy as a bullet will.

After travelling through the rough, over rocks, and down to the trail, we had easy going to the tanks for about four miles, where we arrived at eight o'clock, having been in the saddle eight hours, and having travelled forty-five miles.

We watered the horses first, and then went around to the cow-camp, where we found Billy McU. and wife, with their little three-year-old girl, living in a natural cave. After cooking some coffee and meat and having supper, we turned in, making our beds up outside, the clear blue sky the only canopy over our heads.

We arose at sunlight, washed in the old frying-pan with the handle off, and after a trip around to the tanks to get a couple of pails of drinking-water, we breakfasted on fried meat, biscuit, and coffee. We then helped Jim get his horses ready for a trip up to a spring about fifty miles northeast, where he was going to locate a new cow-camp.

While the boys were getting the pack-horse ready, I took a snap-shot at them. One was standing at the pony's head, holding him; the other two were on either side, tying down the saddle-bags with a lariat.

After Jim's departure we went out to get some "roping" pictures. Tom first chased the steer at full speed, at the same time throwing the rope over his head. After he had caught him and stopped him, he rode around him until the rope bound his feet together. Spurring the pony, he then tripped the steer and threw him to the ground, where the pony held him down by bracing himself and keeping the rope taut. Tom then dismounted, the pony, who was thoroughly trained, meanwhile holding the steer down alone.

Quite frequently a powerful animal has been known to wriggle himself loose and at once attack the horse. After one experience of this sort a pony will exert himself to the utmost to keep the steer down.

The next move Tom made was to take the steer's tail and pass it between his legs. He then, by speaking to the pony, who let go his hold, loosened the lariat and tied the steer's feet together. He was now ready for branding. He then roped another steer, which was thrown by stopping the horse while the steer was running away at full speed.

As it was nearing dinner-time, we returned to camp, and after having some roast beef and coffee we started on a trip up to Sierra Alto, a mountain twenty miles from camp, from the base of which we had a beautiful view of the mountains and plain.

To conclude my story, I will describe our camp and give you an idea of the rocks and caves in our neighborhood.

The rocks are of volcanic origin, and were forced up in the centre of the plain, which is about fifty miles square, and though surrounded by mountains is as level as the sea. The rocks cover about three-quarters of a square mile, and in some places rise perpendicularly to a height of two hundred and fifty feet. They are filled with caves, tunnels, and natural tanks, whence their name.

Our camp was made in one of these caves, which had a roof that was quite flat, and a fire-place in front of the entrance open to the sky above.

The tanks are three in number, and situated in a cañon north of the camp. They are fed with springs which supply an abundance of water for the cattle.

Some of the caves south of the camp were at one time inhabited by Comanches. On the rocks there are still many Indian paintings and drawings, and borings where they used to grind their corn.

There are also many pieces of Indian pottery, and flint chips left from their manufacture of arrow-heads. In one cave that they inhabited there is a natural well, eight feet deep and filled with clear, cool water. In another place there is a deep perpendicular crack from the top of the rock, which is two hundred and fifty feet high, to the plain. It makes a straight passageway for two hundred yards, and averages about four feet in width. During warm weather the prairie rattlesnake makes his appearance in these caves and under the rocks. CARL.

XXVIII.

SANTA FÉ, N. M., *April* 10, 1893.

MY stay in El Paso terminated on Monday last, just three months to a day from the time I said farewell to our beautiful Yonkers.

And on taking leave, I must confess I had a feeling as if I was going away from a dear friend. Many of the guests from the hotel and some of the citizens came to the depot to say good-by, and the leave-taking, hand-shaking, and wishes for good health and happiness, mutually expressed, were as hearty and sincere as if we had lived together for a lifetime.

When I landed in El Paso I was very low down. I was an invalid, and to take a walk of a quarter of a mile was more than I could stand. All this had changed. I had made all my tours through El Paso on foot. To walk three or four miles a day was my regular exercise during the last month or more, whenever the wind was below ten miles an hour.

My long residence in this place gave me many opportunities to meet the citizens. I received nothing but kindness at their hands.

In spite of the rough elements invariably found on the border, life is as safe in El Paso as at home, and all try to make the stay of the visitor as pleasant as possible. My leanings toward the picturesque side of life, and the new scenes which characterized the frontier town and made it especially interesting to me, need not interfere with any visitor. I cannot but recall the look of surprise on the face of the clerk of Uncle Sam's Weather Bureau when I related to him some of the results of my investigations, and told him of the people I had met. The gentleman is from Maine, and he evidently knew El Paso only as he saw it in bird's-eye view from his roost on the highest building in the town.

On leaving El Paso, I can conscientiously recommend it to any one who, like myself, wants rest and sunshine in the winter, a dry atmosphere, and pure, clear air. Should I ever want to emigrate again and bask in the sunshine of a health-giving climate, I will make a bee-line for North Pass City, in Texas, knowing that I shall not be disappointed.

XXIX.

Santa Fé, N. M., *May* 10, 1893.

In my last letter I took leave of El Paso, but I can't help returning to it before I give you a description of my trip to Santa Fé.

Our trunks had been packed a day or two before; my son Carl had brought his saddle from the "corral"; the Mexican curiosities and some fossils he had collected in the mountains had been boxed and started for home, and we were ready to leave. The train was to start at 10.30 A.M., and this left us time enough to make a last visit to Mr. Potter's sanctum. He presented us with a flask of his best whiskey to protect us against the drought which is permanent on the barren plain we had to cross on our way to Santa Fé.

I took a final walk around the basin in the Plaza to say good-by to the alligators, who were taking their morning nap on the water's edge; shook hands with some of the visitors whom I had met, and after having taken leave of our landlord and some of the guests, drove to the depot of the Santa Fé Railroad.

Carl's friends, the boys with whom he had made his equestrian excursions during our stay, all came to say good-by. Some of them had made up a party to travel on horseback through New Mexico to Denver, Colo., and they were going to take a "prairie schooner" to carry the baggage, water, and provisions, and were to leave an hour after our train departed. All were dressed in their travelling costume: broad-brimmed hats, short riding-jackets, high boots, and spurs with rowels the size of a cartwheel.

There was Jim and his brother from Chicago; Dock, the young fellow from New York, who insisted that a part of the camping outfit should consist of silver spoons, knives, and forks; and the remaining "twin." In one of our excursions around El Paso I mentioned two young men from New Jersey, brothers, who looked so much alike that I could only tell them apart when they were together. Although of different ages, we called them "twins." One had started for home about a week previous, and the other was now starting on his first camping-out trip toward the north.

"All aboard!" called the conductor, and with a last waving of hands we left our friends and El Paso behind us.

The train follows for miles the bed of the Rio Grande. We passed the pumping-station which furnishes the town with water from the river when there is any. We took a last look at the old fort, where Uncle Sam has a garrison of some three or four companies of artillery and infantry. To hear the band play and see the soldiers on dress parade, we had visited it many times during our stay.

Within a mile of this point is the smelter, a large establishment with smoking chimneys all over it, where the lead and silver ores, mostly imported from Mexico, are reduced and converted into lead pigs and silver bars. All the laborers are Mexicans, and the works are flanked on two sides by an *adobe* town of the usual type. On our first visit there one Saturday afternoon we found the whole town in an uproar over a football game played by the younger generation, all the men, women, and children forming an admiring audience. Among the lookers-on were two little misses on a pony, who started with us on our return to the city. It was an interesting sight to see how well they kept their seats in the side-saddle, and it gave our horse something to do to keep up with them as they rode along, laughing and chatting and evidently enjoying the race with our buggy.

Our train sped on. The river on our left and the mountains on both sides gradually receded, leaving a plain covered near the water's edge with cottonwood trees, and here and there some fields which surrounded the *adobe* houses of the few Mexicans who raise vegetables and herd cattle on the river bottom.

At Rincon we stopped for dinner. On my return to the train I took a seat in the smoking-car, to enjoy my last Mexican cigar. The car contained a mixed company: drummers from Northern and Western cities, "Greasers," and a few inhabitants who were taking short rides between the way-stations, at all of which our train stopped. As I entered and looked for a seat, I saw a figure dressed in a heavy ulster buttoned up to his chin, above which appeared a woolly head covered with a cap. As I passed I saw a black face with heavy, curling whiskers, and a mustache corresponding to the hair and whiskers. It was an Australian negro, one of a band of six or seven who had given an exhibition of boomerang throwing in El Paso. The poor fellow had met with an accident. After the exhibition there was some kind of a rumpus about the receipts at the gate, and a part of the company seceded and started in on their own hook. I don't know whether the local traditions of Texas as a rebel State had anything to do with this movement, but, at any rate, a part of the performers went to Santa Marcia, the subject of this sketch among them. The financial success of the performance must have been great, because, after the show, our bearded friend got dead drunk, and falling from the stoop of the hotel, broke his arm, and had to be returned to El Paso to have it set and taken care of. I don't know, of course, whether the habit of getting drunk was contracted in the bush in Australia or not, but have my doubts, because, from all accounts, fluids are as scarce in the Australian bush as in Texas and New Mexico; and I am inclined to think it an acquirement of Western civilization, which, no doubt, influences all visitors, whether they come from the antipodes or from nearer home.

A word about boomerangs and their flight. Most of us have thrown boomerangs, figuratively speaking, which hit the thrower with more or less force; but to see these sons of the Australian wilds throw them in reality, is a surprise. We saw a black man, with lean legs and arms that look as if there were no muscles on them, throw the sickle-shaped pieces of wood with a force and skill that caused them to circle over the heads of the spectators who filled the grand-stand of the base-ball grounds of El Paso, to rise like a bird almost out of sight, and to circle in smaller and smaller circuits around the thrower, till they dropped at his feet! It was almost impossible to believe my own eyes, and the experience recalled an anecdote of one of our townsmen who, years ago, when spirit-rapping first came into prominence, related to a friend some of the wonderful feats he had seen. "Well," said this friend, "would you have believed it had you not seen it with your own eyes?" "No," said the relater. "Well, I have not seen it, and that accounts for *my* doubt."

While telling this story we have entered a level plain, more desolate than the plains east of El Paso. Even the sage brush is stunted, and the Mexican dagger-plant and some cacti are the only vegetation that seems to flourish; although, here and there, bunches of short buffalo grass, that looks more like hay, would furnish food for cattle and horses. The river is miles to the westward, and the mountains miles to the eastward, and the drought which has hung over this part of New Mexico for a long time has left many a relic in the shape of skeletons of dead horses and cattle that line the railroad. No evidence of man is in sight for miles and miles on this barren plain, except the windmills for pumping water from wells sunk by some enterprising ranchman.

But such ranches are few and far between, and as we near Lava, about half-way between El Paso and Albuquerque, the desolation becomes more desolate. The sage brush and cactus grow less and less frequent. Black rocks project from each elevation, and gradually the whole plain and the hills, which now approach nearer to the Rio Grande, are covered with them.

Imagine a country without water for miles and miles, where the water to supply the locomotives has to be hauled on tank trains; then look at the black lava jutting out of the loose sand, and you cannot but admire the courage and perseverance of the men who laid the iron ribbon that connects the north pass into Mexico with the west of our great continent.

But the picture changes as if by magic when we approach Santa Marcia. The road runs close to mountains covered from the foot to the top with loose, broken lava. The Rio Grande, furnishing water to a plain spread with flourishing fields, is on our left, the intense green of the alfalfa being interrupted here and there by fields of wheat just sprouting from the ground. Irrigating canals filled with water run in every direc-

tion, their banks lined with trees just putting on their summer coats; the orchards, too, are in full bloom.

Santa Marcia was our next stopping place. Locomotives had to be changed, and we had a few minutes to stretch our legs. The place, as much of it as I could see, is a new American town, but it has its plaza like all the Mexican and Texan towns I have seen. (And I just wonder why we cannot have some such breathing spot in our own beautiful Yonkers!) The principal business houses and hotels are around this plaza. Too late I noticed that some of my fellow-travellers, who had been here before, had laid in a stock of fluid provisions in the shape of a number of bottles of lager, to last until we should reach Albuquerque, our supper station; but I had no reason to regret my neglect when the bottles were opened later on, and a cordial invitation extended to me to join in "irrigating."

A short distance from the town we crossed to the right side of the Rio Grande, and ran through a country where green meadows and ploughed fields cover the valley, and herds of cattle feed on the green plains. The river-bed in some parts is almost dry, the water having been diverted by the irrigating canals, and only a portion returned by soakage through the ground.

Adobe houses line the hills, and in some of the older Mexican towns above the house-tops appear the quaint belfries of the churches, with the bells suspended by ropes from cross-trees. The Mexican has brought his

grape-vines into the valley—fine vineyards of thrifty vines surround like gardens many an *adobe* house.

The mountains have completely changed their character; the lava lining has disappeared, and at times we pass sections in which the vertical walls of red sandstone have been sculptured by the action of water and sand storms into veritable ruins of castles and cathedrals of cyclopean dimensions. The *adobe* houses have also gradually changed color; the sombre gray has given place to a more cheerful red that contrasts pleasantly with the black soil of the valley.

But I had almost forgotten my travelling companions in the smoker.

Our Australian had left us at Santa Marcia, but a group of **travellers had** formed and were carrying on a lively conversation on mining in Mexico. One of them was a cattleman from Colorado returning from a business trip to New Orleans; another was a mining engineer, and the third was a manufacturer from Milwaukee. The two latter had made **a** flying trip **to** Chihuahua, Mexico, to inspect and preëmpt a silver mine of untold richness. I don't remember how much silver to the ton its ore contains, **but it** was fabulous. It was the same story I had heard from the promoters **in El** Paso for months; and even earlier from some **of** my friends at **home who** know something about silver mines in Mexico. The **ranchman thought,** and he said so, that there was more silver in cattle-raising than in all **the** silver mines in Mexico. I think most **of** those who have tried it say the same. From the mine we got to the Mexican, and, at **last, to the** Indian; and I learned, incidentally, that we would pass close to one **of the** Indian "pueblos"—namely, that of Ysleta—and that we would most likely find a number of squaws and youngsters at the station willing to sell us pottery, baskets, and trinkets; so when we stopped I was prepared to step off and see the Indians. I had seen Indians in Michigan and Western New York, dressed up in blankets, beaded moccasons, and all the finery we usually observe in pictures of them; but I was always impressed with the notion that a good part of it was put on for the benefit of the white man—a **sort** of show-dress to attract attention and help sell their wares.

There were about a dozen squaws, boys, and girls, with bright blankets and dressed in a costume of as many colors as you could wish—as pleasing a bit of coloring as I had seen. Some **offered** pottery, jugs, and little plates; others had baskets to sell, and one squaw did **a** flourishing business with her pappoose. The pappoose had on a short blue calico dress **with** a red cloth belt around the waist, and green leggings beaded on **each side on its feet.** She **covered** the baby's face with one corner of her red **striped blanket,** and **called** out : "Nickel, nickel!" The travellers, struck with the novelty of **the** proposition, handed out their nickels, and the squaw **removed the** blanket and showed the baby's face, to the great amusement of the **lookers-** on and to the evident satisfaction of the pappoose, who squalled lustily while its face was **covered.** I think this enterprising mother did the most **business,** and, on the whole, the baby was worth seeing. With its full round cheeks, its small black eyes, and its shining black hair, it was as handsome a child, though rather dark, **as you** would be likely to meet with in many days' travel.

I must confess I was **not very** deeply **impressed** with **the** exhibition; **it** struck me as altogether too theatrical; and yet the ranchman from Colorado, who had visited some of the pueblos in New Mexico, **assured** me that the dresses the Indians wore were nothing more than was customary on festive occasions.

At Albuquerque we had our supper, and as night closed in, I saw no more of the country. We reached Lamy, the junction of the Santa Fé branch road, at 10.30 p.m., and Santa Fé about midnight, and went to bed, thoroughly tired out, at the Palace Hotel.

This is the longest letter I have yet written, but no wonder; there was no place where I could break off, and as Santa Fé weather differs slightly from that of El Paso, I have plenty of time to write, being compelled to stay in the house instead of out-doors, as I did there most of the time.

XXX.

Santa Fé, N. M., *May 16, 1893.*

I HAVE now been here for over a week and have taken a good look at Santa Fé, and I think, although you can find a description of the city and its surroundings in any one of the advertisements of the Atchison, Topeka, and Santa Fé R.R. Co., it will interest you to see it in my company as you did El Paso. And as in that case we climbed up to the Mesa Garden for a view of the city, we will in the present case climb the hill in the rear of the Palace Hotel to the ruins of old Fort Marcy.

But before we start I must remind you not to walk at the same speed as you do at home. You are now nearly eight thousand feet above sea level, and the air is thin; the only safe thing to do is to copy the native Mexicans, who have all the time they want, and never go " faster than a walk," as the signs read on dilapidated bridges.

I thought at first that the reason why the natives did not move any faster was that they had fallen into the same pace as their burros; but I soon found out that even burro speed was too fast for me to keep my wind.

The Palace Hotel fronts on a broad avenue, and opposite is a square covered with buildings used by the garrison for a magazine, wood-yard, coal-shed, etc. We turn to the right of this, and soon reach a cluster of *adobe* houses that line the foot of the hill on which the fort stands. This hill is about two hundred feet high, and following a winding path, we in due time get to the fort and enter from the rear, leaving the ruins of a powder magazine on our left. We now find ourselves in the centre of earth-works covering about an acre of ground; these were the ramparts, and the bastions where the cannon were mounted can still be traced.

We walk to the front and take a bird's-eye view of the capital of New Mexico, the oldest city but one in the United States.

The fort stands upon one of the foot-hills of the Santa Fé Mountains, which tower like giants at the east and extend to the north as far as the eye can reach. But even they are overtopped by old "Baldy," with its head of snow shimmering in the sun. To the westward, two or three ranges of mountains wall in the plain, which extends southerly for miles and miles, to be closed in by another wall of hills still farther distant than those of the west.

The city is situated in a natural basin, protected on all sides from disastrous wind storms; and it is not strange that, long before a European had put foot on the soil of New Mexico, the Pueblo Indians had one of their most populous villages on this very spot. But no trace of the Indian population remains. The Spaniards have civilized and converted them out of existence, and the last vestige of their buildings disappeared forever when the ruins of this pueblo were made over by the government into Fort Marcy, where we now stand. This is historical ground. One civilization has displaced another, and history is repeating itself. As the Indian disappeared before the Spaniard, so the Mexican of the present day is gradually disappearing before the men from the North, and in two centuries from now no more traces of the Mexican will remain in Santa Fé than we find to-day of the Indians.

But let us take a look at the city spread out at our feet. The Federal building, with its flag flying in the breeze, is right in front of us. It stands in a large square surrounded by a stone wall, and in front of the entrance we see the monument erected in honor of Kit Carson, who led the pathfinder, John C. Frémont, to the sunny plains of California.

In front of the Federal building is a wide avenue called Federal Street, and on the other side of the street is New Fort Marcy; but New Fort Marcy has neither ramparts nor bastions. It is bounded by four wide streets and is intersected by a fifth, known as Lincoln Street. This street extends from the Federal building to the palace, and along one side of the Plaza. The headquarters, the parade ground, with its flagstaff and two old brass cannon, the officers' quarters (where the houses occupied by General Grant and General Hayes are pointed out to the visitors), and the barracks face the west side of Lincoln Street, while the magazine and the governor's residence occupy the square on the east side.

The palace, which has served as the habitation of the Spanish viceroy, and, later on, as the dwelling place of the Mexican governors, is now, as said before, the official home of the Governor of New Mexico.

The Stars and Stripes fly at the masthead in the parade ground from sunrise to sunset, and it is a great consolation to see that flag flying when you are away from home in a country as strange looking as that surrounding Santa Fé.

And, while I think of it, I must tell you of something that made rather a queer impression on my mind. A few days ago a new governor was inaugurated in the capital of New Mexico. You may have heard that there was a change of administration at Washington, and this event had to be celebrated.

Two companies of Uncle Sam's "boys in blue," the pupils of the Indian Institute, the patriots of New Mexico who want offices, and others too numerous to mention, marched in procession past our hotel, with banners flying and a band at their head. But imagine my surprise when, for the first time, I saw the defenders of our country adorned with the Prussian helmet! In my boyhood days I had seen them on the other side of the water—the Prussians shooting at us, and we shooting at the Prussians—and I don't wonder now that we got the worst of it, when their helmet has conquered even Uncle Sam. I think old Moltke must feel highly flattered, if he looks down upon us from above, to see his lightning-rod on the top of our boys in blue.

The old palace is an interesting building. It was built in the early part of the eighteenth century, and from our standpoint on the old fort it looks like a long, low house, out of all proportion to its height. In front of the palace is the Plaza, and through the old trees we can just see the roof of the pavilion where the band plays every day, and where Santa Fé promenades every sunny day.

Palace Street is the Fifth Avenue of Santa Fé. Most of the stylish residences line its sides; but a little distance from these I made a discovery. To see the city, you generally go over to the west side of the Santa Fé River, drive up the valley through the Mexican town, and return by Palace Street, after crossing to the east side of the river on a bridge. Well, one day we made this trip, and when within a half mile of the stylish part of the street we discovered on our right a sign with the legend "Santa Fé Beer Garden." We stopped, of course, and found ourselves in the Fatherland. Tables under the trees, and a jolly fellow-countryman of mine ready to serve his customers with pure Santa Fé lager and real St. Louis pretzels. When he brought the lager, however, I was both astonished and amazed. You have, no doubt, seen in Yonkers, in front of the establishments where the juice of King Gambrinus is flowing, a sign with the picture of a tumbler of huge size, saying, "Schooners, five cents." But even the schooners there offered to the thirsty are not to be compared with those of Santa Fé. I could account for it in but one way, namely, the climate here is exceedingly dry, and to moisten the throat it takes a large quantity of fluid. In all my travels I have never met as good measure, except in the Hofbräu, in Munich, Bavaria, where his Royal Highness the King furnishes his thirsty subjects with lager at so much a "stein."

The brick blocks that surround the Plaza are mainly occupied by the sons of Abraham. Here and there modern churches and schools tower above the low *adobe* houses. The cathedral, which is not yet finished, occupies the site of the first Spanish church, and with the Sanitarium—half hospital, half hotel—is on our left; and old San Miguel with its college, the convent of the Sisters of Loretto and its school, bring us gradually to the Santa Fé River. Following the river-bed with our eyes (we cannot follow the stream, because there is little or no water in it), we see to the right and left fields and gardens and house on house in long rows; some of the natural color of the ground, others whitewashed and shining brightly in the sun. On the hill-side at our feet we look into the rear of the houses, and few are without wings on each end, connected by covered spaces like colonnades, where the thrifty housewives can be seen, busy at the washtub.

The Mexican town extends along the Santa Fé valley as far to the south as you can see, and up to as well as into the cañon, where is the reservoir in which the water of the summer freshets (when the snow melts on the Santa Fé range) is gathered to irrigate the valley. The Indian school is in sight at the southwest, and the ruins of the Capitol building, which was destroyed a few years ago, furnish another point for the eye to rest upon.

I have often wondered why in all the towns where prisons are located the inhabitants point with pride to such institutions. Santa Fé has its penitentiary, and it is shown to every visitor who gets in sight of it.

Orchards with budding trees surround the houses, and here and there you can see the irrigating canals winding like silver threads through gardens and fields.

We have seen Santa Fé in bird's-eye view; now let us step down and see it face to face.

The American town is like all others of its kind : brick houses two, three, and even four stories high. Most of the old *adobe* churches have been improved (?) one way and another, so that they are no longer the antique structures I had seen in Juarez. The Mexican himself is no longer the picturesque figure we met with in the south. He has adopted the hat, trousers, and coat of the Americans, and you can see his counterpart any time you take the trouble to look at the Italians in our town. But some color is given to the place by the presence of the officers and soldiers of the post, and now and then by a Pueblo Indian who rides or walks in full dress through the town.

There is "Buckskin" Charley coming down the street. He is a Nambé who sells Indian curios to the guests at the hotels, and is a well-known character. As his sobriquet indicates, he wears buckskin leggings and ornamented moccasons. He sits his black Indian pony as straight as a cavalier. His beaded sash is wound around his waist, and his black hair is held close to his head by a red ribbon.

But let us hurry on and get to the Plaza. The military band is going to play soon, and we shall see the *élite* of Santa Fé in coaches, on foot, and on horseback, promenading the Plaza and the streets that enclose its four sides.

The Governor's Palace, as I said before, is on one side of the square, and the pavilion is near it. From the soldiers' monument in the centre

radiate the paths lined with seats, and the seats are filled with old and young. Señoritas promenade in twos and threes, and the young married couple from the North, who are on their wedding trip, find a seat, not conspicuous, in one of the paths that run at right angles to the streets; they are less used by the promenading beauties. Whole families, fathers, mothers, and children, are seated among the listeners, and all the sunniest seats are filled by dark-skinned Mexicans.

In the surrounding streets carriages drawn by stylish horses and driven by liveried servants keep up their slow walk around the Plaza. Others, less pretentious, follow at the same gait. Gentlemen on horseback join in the

procession, and with these you see some of the visitors who look as if they had never been on horseback before. But the shining light in all this parade is the young lieutenant who has just come from West Point, and who is, by common consent, pronounced the vainest man in all New Mexico.

But let us take a seat in the shade of one of these old cottonwoods. The ground is covered, not with grass, but with bright green alfalfa. The band begins, the coaches and riders gather in front of the palace, and the whole scene is like a dream. I have never listened to good music without a longing for home, so I will stop to have my day-dreams, and we will continue our walk some other time.

XXXI.

Santa Fé, N. M., May 18, 1893.

Like all other tourists, we shall have to see the palace first. The long colonnade extending from Washington to Lincoln Streets forms a sidewalk in front of the building. It is, no doubt, modern, and is ornamented on the edge of the cornice with a low railing, which makes a balcony level with the roof. The western end of this building is used as a post-office, the centre is the official residence of his Excellency the Governor of New Mexico, and the eastern end is occupied by the Historical Society. We will look into the last named.

We first notice in the hallway a part of the trunk of a tree, about three feet in diameter and two feet long, leaning against the wall. Looking a little closer, we discover it to be a petrified tree in which every ring and fibre of wood has been replaced by solid rock. It is the same old tree as when it stretched its giant branches to the sky, but the dead stone has taken the place of the live cells through which the life-giving fluids had circulated long, long ago. I don't know but that this old stump, as a memento of past ages, was very properly placed at the entrance to rooms where the antiquarian of our time tries to preserve the relics left by former generations.

On entering the room, however, we feel disappointed. The collection of antiquities is very unsatisfactory: a few cases of stone weapons used by the Indians before the Spanish conquest, some old Indian pottery, and oil-paintings taken from primitive Indian churches—no doubt the work of pious monks—are about all there is. And the whole is not systematically arranged, but old and new are put on any shelf where there is room.

In an adjoining room is a collection of native minerals of New Mexico; gold and silver ores, soft and hard coal, and even native coke, are represented. But all these specimens are heaped on the shelves in the same way you see piles of stones arranged in a flower-bed to make a mound. A register is kept of all the visitors; so, following the custom, we set down our names and residences, and with civic pride put Yonkers (written large) before New York.

One of the most interesting buildings, next to the palace, is an old house with *adobe* walls four or five feet in thickness, which is claimed to be the oldest in Santa Fé. It is also said that its present inhabitant and owner is a direct and lineal descendant of its builder. It has a baking oven in front, and stands on one of the narrow streets that run substantially parallel to and west of the Santa Fé River, which we had crossed dry-shod to reach the Spanish part of the town.

There is some difference in the look of the houses as compared with those of El Paso; namely, their extreme neatness, and comfortable appearance. We hardly see a window without clean lace curtains and the recess filled with blooming geraniums, which seem to be the favorite flower here.

Each house has its garden, and as planting time is at hand, every one is busy throwing up the ridges which form dikes around the garden-beds, or carefully directing the flow of the water to spread it equally over the surface of each bed, in order to insure an even growth of the grain or vegetable which is to be raised.

The old orchards are in bloom, and I begin to think that, after all, Santa Fé may be the "paradise of fruit growers," as I found it called in a pamphlet prepared by some enterprising land speculator, and freely distributed among the visitors.

About a mile from the ruins of the Capitol (which the charitable people of the city declare was burned down by the people of Albuquerque in order to have the capital of the Territory removed to their town) is the Indian training-school, established some years ago by the United States government.

A large brick building with two wings contains school-rooms and dormitories for about one hundred and sixty boys and girls. These are all ages, from small children to young men and women twenty or more years of age. The scholars in the class-rooms seemed to be highly interested in their studies, and the superintendent assured me that their mental ability was equal to that of white children of the same age. There are Pueblo, Navajo, and Apache children all toiling together under the same roof, and the boys and girls—the boys in military uniform and the girls in neat dresses—showed their training when marching in the procession at the inauguration of the new governor.

Since I have been in this neighborhood I have often thought how nice it would be if I knew some Spanish. When I went to Juarez to see the lottery drawing under the supervision of Colonel Mosby, the lucky numbers were first called out in Spanish, and then, in stentorian tones by the colonel, in English. All legal notices in New Mexico have to be given in Spanish and English, and when the new governor made his inaugural speech an interpreter translated each sentence, as it was delivered, into Spanish.

This continent is inhabited, in the main, by English- and Spanish-speaking peoples, and it looks to me, if any foreign language is of importance to the English-speaking American, it is the Spanish; and I hope you will see if, somehow or other, you can get for this most important of languages a place in the curriculum of our schools.

One feature of the Indian school that deserves special mention is that each boy is taught some trade. There is a carpenter shop, a blacksmith shop, tailoring and shoemaking; and a large area of the prairie on which the school-buildings stand is highly cultivated. All the work is done by the pupils under competent instructors. The girls are equally well taken care of, and those of the pupils who are promoted are sent to Carlisle to finish their education.

I met a young Apache boy who has been in the Indian school for four years and who expects to go to Carlisle shortly. His brother is one of the medicine men of his tribe, and he intends to study medicine as the white men practise it.

XXXII.

Santa Fé, N. M., *May* 20, 1893.

At last the weather has taken a turn for the better. The wind has stopped filling the air with sand, and we have made arrangements to visit the nearest Pueblo Indian village to see what the real Indian looks like at home.

We have a Yonkers colony here; two-thirds of my partner's family and one-third (the biggest, however) of my own. It is unnecessary for me to introduce the travellers, as you are acquainted with them all, except the artist who is the leader in our excursion. He bears the same relation to Yonkers that a witty friend of mine declared, on a certain occasion, I held to the State of Maine.

Several years ago some sons of the Puritans among my acquaintance remembered that they had had forefathers, and concluded to celebrate Forefathers' Day with a New England dinner. Your humble servant was invited, as he supposed, to show the difference between the sons of the early immigrants and the immigrants of the present day. But I found myself at home at once when my friend introduced me to the company as a son-in-law of the State of Maine.

The trip to Tesuque is easily made in one day, and we will select Sunday, as it is a gala day in an Indian village. Our company is a lively one. The boys and girls on horseback take the lead, while the old folks follow in carriages. Ours is drawn by two excellent ponies, named George Washington and Dolly Varden respectively, who travel along at a lively gait.

As we leave the Federal building behind us, we enter a valley in the foothills overshadowed by the Santa Fé range, which, in turn, is overlooked by the snow-clad peak of old "Baldy."

Let us take a glance at the country we are travelling through. Upon the hills on our right and left, stunted pines, and juniper bushes of a deep green, have taken the place of the pale sage brush of the prairie. The mountain sides are covered with a richer growth of pines, through which the white snow is just visible in the less dense parts of the forest; but not a blade of grass or other green thing is to be seen between the bushes; nothing but loose sand everywhere upon the surface of the ground.

As we move along the valley, we find that it is intersected by deep gullies, which have been cut out by the heavy rains that at times fall in this region like cloudbursts. As we gradually approach the level of the foot-hills—the divide between the watersheds of the Santa Fé and the Tesuque rivers—the valley narrows.

The artist calls a halt when we reach the highest point of the divide, and before our eyes, under a deep blue sky, is a panorama that few others can compare with in any part of the world.

On our right the Santa Fé Mountains extend in an apparently unbroken chain for many miles. On our left, but at a much greater distance, another chain of mountains, delicate as a veil, and dotted here and there by patches of snow that shimmer in the bright sunlight, is just visible in the blue mist. In the foreground the foot-hills with their deep green, broken

by the cliff-like rocks that project above them, extend to the point where the two ranges seem to meet. And, away off in the distance, a black butte, with its level top and vertical sides, looks like a mountain surmounted by a fortress. Not a trace of the presence of man is in sight, except the road leading down into the next valley.

But we have seen only a part of the picture; on turning around and looking toward the south we have a landscape of a different type. We can just make out the steeples of the churches in Santa Fé, and the flagstaff with the flag flying on the parade ground of Fort Marcy; and, beyond, the level prairie with scant gray vegetation, extending toward far distant hills colored a deep green. We see the valley of the Santa Fé River, with its long line of adobe houses reaching to the point where the stream disappears among the hills at the right; and the Cerillos Mountains which close in the view. This landscape, bathed in bright morning sunlight, softened by haze in the distance, presents a picture never to be forgotten.

I have seen paintings of mountain scenery by the most celebrated artists, and have often wondered at their strange coloring; yet this view at our feet displayed colors that no artist will ever reproduce on canvas, be he ever so skilful in the use of palette and brush.

The young people have not waited for the old folks, who are admiring the beauty of the scene, and we see them trotting along away down in the valley, now in plain sight, and disappearing again and again behind the bushes by the wayside.

The bed of the Tesuque River, like that of all the streams we have seen in New Mexico, is in a cañon cut deep into the clay that fills the valleys, and the little stream of water that we find seems out of all proportion to its wide bed; yet at times, and not very seldom either, the floods swell the river, and carve deep lines in the high banks on either side.

As we near the cañon of the river, a Mexican settlement comes into view on our right. An adobe church, with its front and belfry whitewashed (the rest of the edifice being the color of the soil), forms the centre of a cluster of adobe houses surrounded by fields and orchards, the latter just beginning to show the first leaves and blossoms. Our road leads down into the river-bed and out again on the opposite side, then up a steep incline to the level land above. The water of the river is carried by a canal near the foot of the hills, at a higher level than the river bottom. Adobe houses in the midst of fruit trees and fields are scattered along the hill-side at our right.

Now we cross a level plain and pass some fruit ranches where the adobe is replaced by the modern brick dwelling, with a bay window made into a veritable greenhouse filled with flowers in full bloom. Neat fences take the place of the rough ones made of cottonwood branches, such as we saw in the Mexican settlement, and brick barns and stables succeed the low *adobe* out-houses.

Here the road follows the curves and bends of the river, now skirting a ploughed field, then a field covered with the stubble of last year's wheat crop, and again winding over a dry plain thickly set with dwarfed pine and low sage bushes. We cross many deep gullies, or arroyos, and occasionally an irrigating canal which furnishes water to the cultivated fields.

One view will leave an indelible impression on my memory. When I left El Paso I had decided to exchange the pen for the brush, and here, before me on the road to Tesuque, I find the very scene to immortalize on canvas. As we descend into an arroyo that leads down to the gully of the Tesuque River it flashes upon our sight.

In the foreground on our right is an ancient cottonwood tree on the edge of the river-bed. The rill of water is lined with alkali, white as the driven snow and interspersed with green plots of grass on which a number of burros are feeding. The far side of the river bottom is lined with green shoots of cottonwood, and behind these ploughed fields extend up the side of the hill. On a plateau half way up the hill-side are a number of *adobe* houses flanked by lots fenced with brush; these in turn are surrounded by stunted pine and juniper bushes scattered over the sandy soil to the top of the hill, where a rough cross planted in a pile of loose stones marks the place where some unfortunate traveller has perished.

It is a picturesque spot, containing in a small compass all the characteristics of the valley: the deep cut which forms the river-bed, the cultivated fields and orchards, the *adobe* houses of that region, and the sombre cross projected on the sky indicating both the faith and lawlessness of the inhabitants.

The picture is not painted, and probably never will be, unless some day, when I have nothing else to do, I should paint it from memory.

We leave this place behind us, and, after some miles travel, Ed points out a white spot on the other side of the Tesuque. As we approach it we can distinguish the whitewashed belfry of a little church in the Indian pueblo. The river bottom is now nearly a quarter of a mile wide, and cattle and goats are frequently seen feeding on the green grass in the river-bed. Our road leads diagonally across it; the church steeple and the dark gray *adobes* become more distinct as we approach. On the left bank of the river are orchards in full bloom. Old trees, testifying to the age of the settlement, shade the houses. On top of the bluff we cross an irrigating canal, and between rows of trees, with ploughed fields on either hand, enter the pueblo of Tesuque.

At the entrance to the village we pass a small house, in front of which a number of squaws are busily engaged making their youngsters presentable. The long black hair of the boys and girls, dripping wet, shines in the sun. The women are already dressed in their national costume, and by their behavior it is plain that a visit from strangers is nothing new. We pass the rear of the church, with its graveyard enclosed by an *adobe* wall. Here and there simple wooden crosses mark the resting places of former generations.

The arrival of our party naturally creates some excitement in the village. Numerous dogs rush out, barking and yelping at the strangers; the inhabitants step to the doors to see what is going on, and the boys and girls gather around our party. The horses are tied to a manger that is supported by forked sticks, and our inspection of the village begins. I will first try to give you a ground plan of the place, and then a more detailed description.

The pueblo proper encloses an oblong plaza, the little church and the governor's house taking up one side; the other sides of the square are occupied by an unbroken line of two-story *adobe* houses, some of which are whitewashed, but most are of the color of the soil.

In my letters I have often attempted to give you a description of the Mexican *adobes*, but an Indian pueblo bears very little resemblance to them, except as to color. The style of building we see here evidently dates back to the time when the square village furnished the best means of defence against the wild Navajos and Apaches, who, from time immemorial, have robbed and plundered the peaceful village Indians.

The outside of the square building—a vertical wall two stories high—could be easily defended, and the square enclosed, should an enemy obtain entrance, presents an equally good protection against attack.

The village house is two stories high, but the side facing the enclosure is only one story high, and a roof, or gallery, covering about one-third of the lower floor, extends all around the front. The wall which separates the first row of rooms is carried up two stories, and so are the third and rear walls, forming, as it were, three rows of rooms on the ground and two on the second story.

As we now see the buildings, the rooms on the lower floor are entered from the court, and those on the second floor from the gallery; but in olden times those on the ground floor were also entered from above.

To reach the gallery they have a number of ladders made of rough timber and long enough to extend six or eight feet above it; they lean, at intervals, in front of and against each dwelling. The rungs, being from sixteen to eighteen inches apart, are not the most convenient of stairs to climb, and I was very much amused at the sight of two squaws helping a little girl of three or four years up one of these ladders. The squaw above, having hold of one of the child's hands, was pulling, and the one below was pushing, while the little one hung on like a spider to a web, but was hardly able to reach from rung to rung.

Our arrival, as was said before, brings the greater part of the population to the doors and the edge of the gallery. We make our first call on the governor of the pueblo at his house, which is next to the church and

separated from the main building by one of the entrances. He has just completed his toilet. His coal-black hair is cut in the shape of a bang on his forehead, and the rest hangs like the mane of a pony on each side of his face down to his belt. He wears buckskin leggings and a flannel shirt, and speaks English fairly. As we enter his dwelling the first objects to attract our attention are three curved stones on which the squaws, even of this day, grind the corn for their bread.

In a roomy fire-place is a girl in Indian dress, including leggings, her long hair almost covering her back down to the waist, baking *tortillas* (corn-cakes) on a heated stone. On the earthen floor the skin of a cow is spread, and upon it lie the remains of the carcass of a heifer, around which a small, snarling cur is prowling, but he does not seem to dare to help himself to it.

Adjoining is the living and bed-room, lighted at the extreme end by a small window. It has a small fire-place in the centre, on one side of which is a settee made of a number of rolled-up blankets, and on them sits the wife of the governor, nursing her pappoose. Two older people are seated near her, and a number of youngsters who have entered with us help to fill the low room. In one corner we notice a beam suspended from the ceiling, on which is displayed the finery of the family, consisting of various articles of Indian manufacture, such as squaw dresses, Navajo blankets, and belts and sashes of divers colors. Our host exhibits a number of war clubs, loaded with a stone at the butt end and ornamented with horse tails at the other, which he offers for sale.

The two rooms are as clean as a pin and neatly whitewashed, and, after we have made some purchases, we are shown into a third—evidently a storeroom—where dried meat and hides of cattle and goats are hanging from the ceiling. One of the squaws brings out a big basket full of idols made of baked clay, and another basket filled with small pots and plates, from which we make some selections, and then step out to visit the main building.

In the square we find two or three dozen Indian children, some of them having pappooses wrapped in blankets or rags tied to their backs. The edge of the gallery is lined with men, women, and children, most of them as well dressed as those we saw at Ysleta. Bright colors predominate, and one young squaw reminds me of a picture of "Rebecca at the Well" that I had admired so often when a boy—it was in an old Bible. The picture represented a young woman with an earthen jar gracefully balanced on her head. Just as we step out of the goveronr's house we see a young squaw passing—evidently just returning from the irrigating canal—with an urn-shaped jar upon her head. Approaching one of the ladders, she ascends it, keeping the jar balanced, and walks along the gallery to one of the doors, where, taking hold of the jar with both hands, she lifts it off and then enters.

We are invited to visit the artist who makes the idols. He goes to work for our benefit to show us how it is done, and I must say it is remarkable how quickly the lump of clay in his hands assumes the quaint shape of the conventional Pueblo Indian idol, with its large head and open mouth, its short arms holding a little pot, and its crooked legs encircling the bottom. The room is well lighted and whitewashed, and the rear wall ornamented with pictures of the Crucifixion and the saints.

As we want some Indian vases, we will climb one of the ladders and enter the rooms above. Here an old squaw exhibits a lot of her ware, assisted by a younger one, evidently her daughter, who speaks a little English. We price some of the wares, and the young squaw offers them for a "quarter"; but when we agree to take them at that figure, the old woman says something, either in Pueblo or Spanish, to the younger one, and taking hold of the vase, says: "Half a dollar." She has raised the price, but we carry them off at that figure.

In another house we are shown some squaw dresses of their own weaving, such as they wear at their dances; but these are not for sale, being heirlooms that date back for generations in the families of their owners.

Almost every house is provided with an oven for baking bread and pottery. They are usually located before the house, or on the gallery in front of the entrances to the rooms in the second story, and they look like clay bee-hives of mammoth dimensions.

The village and the people give an impression of contentment and thrift such as I have never received elsewhere, and the cleanliness of the people and the houses is the direct opposite of what one might expect from the descriptions given by those who had visited some of the tribes farther north.

This pueblo contains from fifty to sixty people, who cultivate their land and raise cattle, goats, and burros, like their Mexican neighbors, but retain with the utmost tenacity the habits and customs of their forefathers.

After a stay of some hours we start on our return, making a halt after crossing the Tesuque River, as the horses must be watered and the travellers also feel the need of some refreshment. Our carriage has been well stocked with provisions, so we will sit down on the bank of the stream, with the gray Indian *adobe* before us, flanked by blooming orchards on the right and left, and the high Santa Fé range behind us, and we will enjoy the view and the lunch in equal proportions.

XXXIII.

SANTA FÉ, N. M., *May* 19, 1893.

As our trip to Tesuque, and the sights we saw, simply served to increase our interest in the Pueblo Indians, San Ildefonso, another pueblo twenty-four miles away, in the valley of the Rio Grande, was selected as our next point to visit.

A few days before we started on this trip I had made the acquaintance of one Facundo Sanchez and his family, who had given all of us a cordial invitation to visit them at their home in San Ildefonso.

The house of Mr. Deming, the artist, is a sort of headquarters for all the Indians who visit Santa Fé. He has lived with the Indians for years in the Northwest, and has also, as he says, been a "boarder" in Sitting Bull's tepee for a whole hunting season; and his opinion of the Indian differs slightly from that expressed by General Sherman. Ed is an enthusiastic admirer of the red man, and looks upon the treatment of his red brothers as the greatest crime ever committed by our government.

Sanchez had two sons in the Indian school, and was on a visit with his wife and pappoose to see the youngsters. When I entered the room where he and his family were seated, I was particularly struck with the pleasant reception I had from both Sanchez and his wife. They knew that they were in the house of a friend, and felt as much at ease as if they were in their own home at San Ildefonso. They were dressed in their national costume, and the smiling face of the mother, although she understood not one word of English, bore as pleased a look when we noticed the little pappoose as would that of the most cultivated white woman.

The Pueblo Indian has long since passed the stage where the women are simply the servants and beasts of burden of the "masters of creation." He tills the ground and tends the cattle while the squaw takes care of the house and the children.

The two Indian boys were dressed like white boys and looked bright and intelligent, and they took a great deal of interest in the paintings of Indian scenes scattered about the room.

Among the Indian curiosities were a bow and a quiver filled with arrows, which at once attracted their attention. They took them from the hook, and the elder boy tested the bow with his fingers. In the rear of the house is a yard, and to please the boys as well as ourselves we threw out a pasteboard box a distance of forty feet, and watched with interest while they shot at it. The box was not more than six inches square, yet twice out of three times the elder boy would send his arrow through it, while I could barely succeed in shooting an arrow as far as the box.

Sanchez spoke English well, so during luncheon and afterward I talked with him about village government, the crops, and irrigation on the reservation, and found him an intelligent and well-informed man. He now tendered his invitation, which was of course accepted, and early one morning shortly afterward we started on our journey.

The trip being too long to admit of taking the ladies, our party was reduced to four. Our carriage was drawn by the two trusty ponies, "George Washington" and "Dolly Varden." The artist and the amateur cow-boy occupied the front seat, and my venerable partner and myself the back one.

The road to San Ildefonso is the same one that we travelled over when going to Tesuque, but we stayed on the right side of the river, leaving Tesuque on the left. The valley begins to widen here, and we see the industrious Pueblos ploughing their fields and attending to their irrigating canals.

A field as level as a table, with a bare-headed Indian holding in a furrow a wooden plough of primitive construction drawn by a burro, is a novel picture to a traveller who has heard all his life of the Indian only as a wild man of the woods, with tomahawk in hand, scalps in his belt, and murder in his eye.

The Tesuque reservation is quite extensive. Good farming and grazing lands are on either side of the river-bed and in the arroyos in the Santa Fé Mountains. But as we move on, the country becomes wild, the mountains recede, the valley broadens; red sandstone, fantastically carved, lines the hill-sides or projects above the pine-covered hillocks. The plain in the valley assumes to a greater or less extent the characteristics of the prairie.

Before we started from Santa Fé we had equipped our carriage for a trip in the wilderness. Rifles, shot-guns, and revolvers formed the armament, and in cans, bottles, and bundles we carried our provisions. The younger men were on the outlook for game, but had so far been unsuccessful, when two owls, of the kind that live with the prairie-dogs and the rattlesnakes, flew up on our right. Both the artist and the cow-boy jumped from the carriage to kill them. The artist was ahead, and with two shots from his gun slew both birds, and thus added two more specimens to the collection of the cow-boy.

But imagine our excitement when what we all thought to be a gray wolf crossed our path. Our road was leading up a gentle incline between two hills, when this animal crossed it a short distance before our horses. He had evidently been over to the valley to get some breakfast, and was on his way to his lair in one of the gullies or arroyos when we saw him. I tell you he looked handsome as he trotted off and disappeared behind the low sand hill on our right.

Carl grasped his rifle and jumped out on one side, Ed his revolver and jumped out on the other, and even my partner took his gun and ran after the wolf. (Henry had been a great hunter when a boy, and I guess his old love for hunting returned and carried him off.) All at once I found myself alone. All three had disappeared over the knoll. I heard a sort of a thud, but could not believe it was a shot, so I took it easy. The sun was shining brightly on the sand, the supply of liquid provisions was ample, and as I never had any ambition in that line, I felt entirely satisfied to sit there as quartermaster and let the others chase the wolf.

And this reminds me of an incident of my boyhood which may have something to do with my—aversion, I was going to say—to killing things.

When I was a boy ten or twelve years old we had in our little village as minister an enthusiastic botanist. He was also a great French scholar, and for a number of years he tried, very unsuccessfully however, to hammer French grammar into my cranium. I suppose he did the best he could in that line; but when it came to the flowers in the fields and the birds in the woods, his lessons bore more fruit than in the other line. I began to collect plants, birds' eggs, and insects; and when, later on, I received instruction in the art of stuffing birds and beasts, my natural history collection took all my spare time, and even during vacation I was busy from morning till night arranging and perfecting it. I bothered all

my friends to shoot specimens for me to stuff, until one day, when my father was going to the woods, he said: "Why don't you shoot your own specimens?" This was an idea that had never occurred to me, so I took a single-barrelled shotgun I had owned for years and went along.

The valley in which our little farming village nestled was enclosed by hills covered with thriving vineyards at the foot and low brushwood on the top. The first bird I saw, a lark, was perched upon a pole to which the grapevines cling. I fired and killed it. My excitement was so great that I dropped the gun, picked up the bird, and running to my father showed it to him. "Where is your gun?" he asked; after some searching I found it in the bushes where I had fired at the lark.

The gun was reloaded, and we started on. After a while I noticed a chippy hopping about in a low green bush, and concluded to bag it also. I fired and hit the bird, but did not kill it. I had shattered both wings and mortally wounded it, no doubt; but as I took it up in my hands it looked at me with such mournful eyes that I have never forgotten it, and it was the last time I ever fired at or killed a bird.

But to return to the wolf hunt. Soon things got to be tiresome, and I concluded to follow the footprints of the wolf up the hill. They were plainly to be seen in the loose sand, and he must have been a big fellow. I followed the trail up the hill and around the top for about one hundred yards, when all trace of it disappeared. I marked the last footprint, and then pursued the tactics of the Indian, of whose sagacity I had read so much, and circled around the mark at a short distance, examining the sand; but no more footprints could I find, and I gave it up as a bad job and sat down on top of a sandstone butte that projected above the hill. There, right in front of me, were the hills and arroyos of the Santa Fé range, and way on top, some hundreds of feet above me, the form of a solitary hunter, looking, as I had, for a trace of our wolf.

All at once I heard a shout. A long distance off the artist and the cow-boy had spied me from the top of a sandy butte. They had found the wolf dead under a juniper bush half a mile away. At the spot where I had been looking for the wolf, he had been shot by Carl with his rifle, and the jump he made when hit had carried him so far that I lost all trace of him.

The hunters with their trophy came along after a while, puffing and blowing like porpoises. The hot sun and thin atmosphere had taken away their breath; and, what was worse, the gray wolf turned out to be a coyote, a much smaller and less ferocious animal, but, still, game not to be despised.

While the hunters followed the wolf, and I sat on the sandstone butte, a lot of Mexicans had passed our carriage, and I did not notice them until they had gone some distance beyond it. When the hunters returned and in great distress inquired for the "Blue Grass," it was gone. Without doubt the Mexicans had annexed our flask; but after a careful search it was found under the seat, where it had slipped during the excitement when all but myself jumped from the carriage. So, with a mental apology to the Mexicans, the flask passed around, and all felt highly elated because we four had killed a wolf.

Another specimen had been added to the collection; and although I myself failed to find his trail, I had discovered not a great ways from the hill-top a lot of broken pottery, the remains of a jar. It was in a portion of country that seemed to be a wilderness; it looked so desolate that you could not imagine that anybody had ever lived there; yet here were the pieces of pottery, proving conclusively that the Pueblos had had a habitation not far away.

Highly pleased with our success, we go on. The country is growing wilder as we advance; on our right the hills and mountains, with their sandstone cliffs, grow higher and higher, while on our left the plain is furrowed by deep cañons cut into the thick soil of the valley.

By and by we reach a Mexican settlement. The valley had descended gradually, and a new irrigating canal could take water from the river-bed. Numerous curs receive us with their snarls, and señoritas look out of the doors at the strangers.

Fields and orchards take the place of the desert plain in the valley of the Tesuque. The excitement of the wolf hunt had distracted our attention from the scenery. We are nearing the mountain chain that we saw, enveloped in a blue mist, from the divide. The butte, rising a thousand feet above the plain, is on our right hand, but the blue mountains on the other side of the Rio Grande are in front and seem to close in the Tesuque valley. The patches of snow on the mountain sides look out of place in the warm sunshine, and it is difficult to destroy the illusion which the rocky cliffs produce—that they are the ruins of dwellings built by a race of giants ages ago.

The Indian village of San Ildefonso is located in the fork of the Tesuque and Rio Grande rivers. The pueblo is almost hidden by the green trees that line the irrigating canal. Herds of cattle and goats, tended by Indian boys, are scattered over the plain, and in the fields we see men busily engaged in irrigating the land and carefully guiding the water over the surface. The laborers are at work in rather scant dress, or undress: a flannel shirt, a ribbon tied around the head—that is all!

We enter the village from the east and find ourselves in an oblong plaza, with rows of one and two storied *adobes* on three sides, and a church, with a wooden cross in front, occupying a fourth side. The same style of ladders, the same ovens, and the same people we had seen in Tesuque meet us here.

We stop in front of the house of our friend Sanchez, and are received with smiles by his wife, he being away looking after his fields. His is a one-storied house, with a gallery or veranda running the whole length of the building. It is raised one step above the ground, and the roof is supported by rough columns of cottonwood. Bright, clean windows light the interior, and here, as in Tesuque, the doorsill is raised six or eight inches above the floor—as I have seen it in the houses of the wood-cutters in the forests of Bohemia. The room we enter is evidently the sleeping apartment. The pelts and blankets which serve as beds are rolled up, and make a settee running the whole length of one side of the room; and on a blanket spread out in front of this impromptu settee sleeps the little pappoose we have seen in Santa Fé.

An adjoining room, furnished with a table, some chairs, and a bedstead, was put at our service. The boys soon had all our baggage and provisions in proper shape, and then the important piece of work, the skinning of the wolf, is next in order. With the assistance of a young Indian, while dozens of youngsters looked on, the job was quickly under way.

The horses have been unhitched and taken to the stable, the carriage unloaded, and the harness hung upon pegs built into the *adobe* walls, and we are ready to take a walk about the place while our hostess is busy cooking the dinner. A few cottonwood trees planted here and there are the only signs of vegetable life in the square. Close by is a shed under which an old Indian is engaged in fitting a helve into an axe. Every once in a while he swings the axe and makes a cut into the log on which he has been sitting, and then goes at the handle again, cutting off some more, or smoothing it to make it easy to his hand.

We take a walk over to the church at the other end of the square. It is like all the others we have seen. The front wall is carried up like the gable to a house with a pitched roof, and in two openings in this wall the bells are suspended, while a wooden cross surmounts the highest peak. The church is closed, and as we stroll on we reach the ruins of a structure, no doubt a church much older than the one in use at present. The roof has disappeared, but the enclosing wall remains, and the carved girders, together with the carved wooden columns that support them, are well preserved. The ornamental carving upon these is of the same style I had seen in the cathedral at Juarez, and was, no doubt, the work of some pious monk who had helped to convert the heathen Indian to Christianity.

Between this interesting ruin and the Rio Grande are some fields. It is planting time, and the male population is busy ploughing or irrigating the land. The Rio Grande, a real stream here with water in it, flows peacefully along, its shores lined with woods or meadows dotted with grazing cattle, as far as the eye can reach. To the left, extending from the river bank to the foot of the sand hills—a distance of a mile or so—we see cultivated fields and green trees, with *adobe* houses resting in their shade.

To investigate the fields surrounding the village we take a walk outside of the pueblo proper. A street extends from the village houses, and here, unexpectedly, we come upon the council chamber.

The council chamber was in olden time the centre of the religious and social life of the pueblo. The old men of the tribe met there to consult together upon matters of government, and the medicine men and priests performed their services to the Great Spirit within its walls. But the council chamber even to-day has lost little if any of the importance it had before the church at the other end of the square was erected and the cross raised upon its belfry.

It is a circular *adobe* building, partly underground, and can be entered only from above. *Adobe* stairs lead up to the flat roof, which is surrounded

7

by a wall two or three feet in thickness and as many feet high. Two poles project above a square opening in the roof. We descend the ladder, and find ourselves in a room lighted only by the opening through which we have entered. It takes some time before our eyes become accustomed to the darkness and we are able to see the interior. We can make out the rough column in the centre which supports the roof, and the heavy round log, acting as a girder, extending from side to side, and embedded, like the rafters, in the thick walls. Then we see a square fire-place, and the only furniture of the room, a seat which is merely a projection of the wall about two feet in height. The chamber is at least forty feet in diameter. There are two round holes in the wall, opposite each other, one near the ground, the other near the ceiling; but though they may ventilate they do not help to lighten the gloomy room.

It is a remarkable structure, unlike anything I have ever seen or heard of, and there is no doubt that it was used by Pueblo Indians long before the white man put foot on their soil.

As we leave the council chamber, an old man by signs invites us to enter his house. Two squaws are at work making pottery—large vessels that would hold more than a gallon. One of them is smoothing and polishing a sun-dried jar, while the other, squatted on the ground, is shaping another on a stone in front of her. No wheel or tools are used. The soft clay is built up, and then with one hand inside and the other outside she deftly forms a circular vessel, so regular in shape that a superficial observer would think it had been made on a potter's revolving table.

We add a few samples to our collection of Indian pottery, and return across the square to the house of Sanchez, where we find the skinning of the wolf completed, and dinner ready.

In a corner of the guest chamber is a fire-place in which our hostess has built a wood fire, cooked a beefsteak in a pan supported by a tripod, and brewed coffee in a tin pot. These, with canned vegetables and other good things, made a feast fit for the gods. We had left Santa Fé early in the morning, and it was late in the afternoon before we reached San Ildefonso.

While we were taking our walk and refreshing the inner man we had a whole drove of youngsters around us. The white man here is evidently as interesting to them as they were to us, and they were made exceedingly happy when Deming distributed a bag full of apples among them.

While eating our lunch I accidentally looked out of the window, and saw that another crowd of youngsters, older than those in the house, were making faces at the back of our carriage. No doubt one of them had discovered that the smooth, well-varnished carriage reflected their faces, and the whole troop had no end of fun. It is surprising, however, how these youngsters carry others on their backs. At least one-third of those who were laughing and scampering around the carriage had pappooses tied on their shoulders. But it did not seem to interfere in the least with their movements, and the pappooses never squealed, even when tossed up by their carriers to get them a little higher upon their backs.

Shortly after dinner Sanchez came in and took us in hand to show us all there was to be seen. We took another walk about the place, but could not get into the church. The priest was away, as he did not come to the pueblo but once or twice a month. "Is he one of your own people, or a Mexican?" I asked. "Neither," said Sanchez; "he is some Frenchman or Irishman, I don't know." Yet Sanchez's house was decorated with religious pictures like the rest.

He also informed us that the next day they were to have a dance, and if we stayed over we might witness it. Now, here was a predicament; the young fellows, of course, wanted to stay, and after taking another look at the nice clean room, the old folks concluded to do the same. When we left home we did not know but that we might stay over night at the pueblo, and we had brought blankets enough to camp out with; but it proved an unnecessary precaution, as our hostess was well provided with Navajo blankets, and my partner and I being old soldiers, we preferred a bed upon the clay floor to the bedstead, which seemed not strong enough to support the weight of two such heavy men.

But there was a surprise in store for us. When the sun went down the Indians came in from the fields, and preparations were made to practise the dance that evening in the "council house," and we were invited to be present. Sanchez and his wife were to participate, one as a chanter, the other as a dancer.

Shortly after dark we started for the council house. A thick cloud of smoke was coming out of the hole in the roof through which we were to enter. Right under this hole was a wood fire which furnished the only light there was, and it seemed like entering the lower regions as we descended the ladder with uncertain steps amid a heavy cloud of dense smoke.

The smoky atmosphere, the sound of the drum accompanied by the monotonous chant of the singers, the two rows of dancers revealed by the flickering light of the fire, made up a scene as uncanny as the dance Tam o' Shanter saw in Alloway Kirk when his Satanic Majesty led the orchestra.

As our eyes get used to the light, we see a little more clearly the rows of dancers, facing each other and keeping time with their feet to the beat of the drum. A man and a woman, a man and a woman, eight or ten on a side, each carrying green branches in their hands, and swaying to the right and the left as the two lines at times slowly approach and then recede from

each other. At other times the two lines pass each other in the middle, changing sides like the dancers in a set of the Virginia reel.

On the seat running around the chamber is seated the audience of men, women, and children, but the darkness at that distance from the fire is so deep that we see only the merest outlines, and but little more of the dancers. The sight was more weird than the liveliest imagination could ever produce.

We left before the dance was concluded. The smoky hall, after our long ride, reminded us that we needed rest, and we soon retired, fully convinced that the sight we had just seen had been viewed by few other visitors to an Indian pueblo.

After a good night's sleep, we awoke in the morning and took a walk to see the surrounding scenery. From our host we learned that there is a tradition that long ago his people had their village on the butte we had seen from the divide, but it was such a long time ago that even the trail leading up to it had disappeared.

In this clear atmosphere the mountains on the other side of the river seem to be within a stone's throw, yet they are miles away. The ragged sides cut up by deep valleys, the tops crowned with bold rocks, some overhanging the vertical walls; the patches of snow, interspersed here and there by scanty growths of pines, with the bright morning sun illuminating every projecting point; the peaceful Indian village with its adjacent fields and gardens, the river flowing at our feet—all combined to make a picture grand and impressive to the beholder.

Our Indian friend next took us to the irrigating ditch and explained their system of watering the fields, and how the "governor" and the old men regulated the affairs of the pueblo. "How much land have you in your reservation?" I asked. "We have land on this side and on the other," said he, "and since the government is in the East they cannot take it away from us any more."

It seems that while Mexico controlled the country the right of the Indian to the soil was never recognized, and their lands were taken from them by the Spanish and Mexican settlers without much ceremony; and there is evidently not much love lost between the two races to-day, although they live next door to each other.

Deming is in full sympathy with the Indians. He feels very sore yet about the loss of one of his horses, which was stolen, on his last trip to the Apache and Navajo reservation, from his camp near a Mexican settlement.

Our guide had left us some time before to join the party who were to participate in the dance, when the slow beating of a drum reminded us that it was time to return to the plaza.

Near one of the trees we found a group of men, our host among them, chanting in a monotone in time with the beats of the drummer. They stood facing each other and forming a circle, while the drummer, outside of the ring, faced a group of men and women who were dancing.

The sight we had seen the evening before had prepared us for the present one. We viewed it then, as it were, in a cloud, while now the sunshine brought out light and shadows to the astonished lookers-on.

The green branches and wreaths furnished the predominating color, and the dresses of the squaws, the painted skins of the men, the rhythmical motion in time with the chant, and the drum completed the scene.

The dancers, about twenty in number, half of them squaws and the other half men, danced as they had in the council room, in two rows facing each other; and I must not forget two youngsters, a boy and a girl, ten or twelve years of age each, who evidently were receiving their first instructions in the ceremony.

The chanters and the drummer wore their every-day dress—leather leggings and flannel or cotton shirts; their long hair was tied tightly around the head with a red ribbon or red handkerchief; but the dancers were in dance costume.

Let me try to give you a description, and, as our hostess is one of the performers, let me describe her costume. She, like all the other squaws, was barefooted. A long dark dress, or rather bag, reaching a little below the knee and drawn over the right shoulder, the left being bare, is fastened by a broad red sash around the waist. The sash is tied in a knot on the right side, and its long tassels reach almost to the ground. It is a fine specimen of weaving, diagonal figures of lighter color running through the centre. She also wears a number of necklaces, and from one depends a silver cross. To describe her head-dress, however, is not an easy matter. It is a thin board fitted to the head from ear to ear, and projects upward in three points a foot or more above the head. It is decorated with feathers and fastened by strings under the chin. In her right hand she holds a bunch of green twigs, and in her left a string with little tin rattles that jingle at every movement. All the squaws wear the same head-dress, and their gowns differ but little. Some are more, others less, ornamented on their upper or lower edges. The belts or sashes differ in shade and color, but the same description will do for all. The men wear moccasons adorned with skunk-skin trimmings, and a cotton skirt, held by a broad sash of unbleached cotton about the waist, and reaching down to the knee. The broad sash, like that of the women, is tied on the right side, and the long tassels almost touch the

ground. But the sash also holds a fox skin, which hangs down behind, the fox's tail and hind legs swinging and swaying with each motion of the wearer. The chest and arms are bare, but numerous white spots form lines from the waist to the shoulders and down the chest. Other dots extend from the shoulders to the hands. Bunches of green cottonwood twigs are fastened by leather armlets to the upper arm, and another bunch to the top of the head. In the right hand they carry rattles made from a gourd, and in the left green branches.

The dance is the spring or planting dance, and, no doubt, dates back to a time when it was performed to propitiate the Great Spirit and to induce him to give fair weather to plant the crops. It was an acted prayer. And the Indian squaw of to-day, with a rosary around her neck and a cross on her breast, still worships her old gods.

To portray the motions of this group is, however, beyond my power. The feet are lifted alternately from the ground; the branches are in motion; the bodies sway forward and backward in unison with the weird chant and the beat of the drum. Slowly the procession moves along; the chanters have formed in two lines, with the drummer ahead, following the dancers, who have closed up and formed in couples, two bucks and two squaws alternately. The first part of the ceremony is over, and the actors in it retire, climbing a ladder to the upper story of one of the houses on the other side of the square.

It is nearly noon and time to get under way if we want to reach Santa Fé by daylight. Our horses are hitched; we say good-by and leave the pueblo, this time fully convinced that what we had seen had not been a theatrical performance.

I must relate yet another incident of the day before. After we had made up our minds to stay over night we went hunting for Indian curiosities. We found some blankets, leggings, squaw dresses, and other wearing apparel of Indian manufacture. One of the squaws brought out a cradle of very ancient date, as proved by the wear of the rawhide straps by which it had been suspended from the ceiling. After the purchase was made Carl pointed to the pappoose in her arms and asked, "*Quanto por este?*" (How much for it?) The squaw looked at him in astonishment and hugged the baby tightly in her arms, but when her first surprise was over she started into a loud laugh, in which the people, young and old, joined heartily when she told them that Carl wanted to buy the pappoose to put in the cradle.

There is evidently a good streak of humor in that pueblo, and I can imagine how they must have laughed in their sleeves when they had sold their old trumpery to the white men for more than it was worth.

On our way back the young men had plenty of sport shooting wild doves and quail, and this delayed us so that the sun was sinking in the west as we neared Tesuque.

We had seen the Santa Fé range in the morning with the sun in the east. When the sun now neared the horizon, the snow on old "Baldy" and on the caps of the other mountains began to glow and assumed a light red hue, which gradually changed to a deep purple as the sun went down, leaving the high tops in the starlit night looking like tall black walls enclosing the valley.

We reached Santa Fé an hour after sun-down, and had to trust to our ponies to carry us safely by the deep cañons up to the divide and down into the valley again.

XXXIV.

Santa Fé, N. M., *May* 25, 1893.

We are again on the road, and our objective point is San Domingo, the largest pueblo in the immediate neighborhood of Santa Fé. Our trip is southward over the prairie. While passing the Indian school we see the boys at play, and one youngster with bow and arrow hunting prairie-dogs. The latter are very numerous about here. I saw them to-day for the first time in their natural state, popping up from their burrows, sitting bolt upright and looking at the passers-by, then disappearing in the twinkling of an eye into the ground, to reappear a second later, the head only protruding from the hole, watching and waiting till the coast is clear. Hundreds of their hills are scattered over the plain, some close by the road, others partly hidden behind the sage brush; and we see the little animals running and scampering about everywhere. As it is early morning, they are out for their breakfast. But right there on the top of a fence is a large hawk who is out also for something to eat. He is intently watching the rodents, when a well-aimed shot brings him to the ground—another specimen of New Mexican birds.

The ride over the prairie is a monotonous one, varied only by the sight now and then of a cotton-tail rabbit or a pair of wild doves, which furnish sport for the two hunters on the front seat of the carriage. The level plain gradually changes into a rolling surface. In the depressions green grass is seen occasionally, and as we near the foot-hills of the Cerillos Mountains we find flocks of sheep, numbering many hundreds, feeding on the scant herbage.

The Cerillos are famous for their mineral wealth, and we see the miner's footprints on every side. On the level surface and on the sides of the pine-covered hills are shafts and tunnels, dug by prospectors in search of gold and silver.

We pass some of the abandoned mines. The wooden houses and derricks stand just as the promoters left them when, after a thorough investigation, the ore was found to be unprofitable.

We enter the mountain range through a narrow pass, and find ourselves at once in a wilderness of perpendicular rocks and deep arroyos. The road at times is barely wide enough for us to pass around some projecting rock on one side while a deep cañon is on the other. In about the centre of the range we reach Bonanza, an abandoned mining town, which but a few months ago was full of life and business. But the stamps, mills, and smelters are closed, boards are nailed over the windows, and we see but one living inhabitant.

He is seated on the window-sill of a little frame building with the sign "Post-office" over the door. Evidently all the others had left in despair, but the postmaster had remained to draw his salary, which, no doubt, is an extravagant one and worth holding on to. It is a depressing sight to see an abandoned town—the houses and buildings showing no signs of life, no smoke arising from the chimneys, and the whole place looking like a burying ground with its monuments to the departed.

From Bonanza the road gradually descends to the valley of the Calisteo River. As we approach it, the cañon we are travelling in grows deeper, and the rugged sides close in, so that where the road leads out of it, the almost vertical walls rise hundreds of feet above our heads. Our road in the cañon is the bed of a mountain stream which discharges its waters into the river, and we soon find ourselves in a cut from ten to fifteen feet deep and a hundred wide—the dry river bed of the Calisteo.

Our ponies climb the opposite bank, and we come out on the level surface of a wide valley, and see right in front of us the town of Cerillo, a station on the Atchison, Topeka and Santa Fé Railroad.

We had made a trip over hill and dale of more than twenty miles, and the sight of a sign—"Anheuser-Busch"—on one of the houses was like seeing an oasis in a desert. But imagine our surprise when, on entering the establishment, we found a fully equipped *lunch counter* in the rear, and the feeling of relief we experienced when a well-done plate of ham and eggs, garnished with a schooner of lager, was set out to refresh the inner man.

Our equipment attracted a good deal of attention. We had a regular battery of guns and rifles and a full supply of blankets, and one old man, evidently a miner, after looking it all over said, as he turned away: "I suppose you fellows thought you were to go on a bear hunt when you came over here."

The best road to San Domingo is by the river bed, and a quarter of a mile from Cerillo we entered it. The bed of the Calisteo is of the same character, but much larger, and the grotesquely carved clay banks much higher than the bed of the Tesuque.

For miles and miles we drove on. At times a small stream of water is trickling in circuitous line over the river bottom, covered with a thick layer of alkali, white as snow.

Once in a while we would find a trail down the steep bank, where cattle and horses made their way from the level above to the ditches filled with soapy water; but before long all traces of water disappeared, and the bed, now several hundred feet wide, twisting and turning to the right and to the left, is covered with a fine loose sand, piled up here and there, and blown by every gust of wind, forming ridges like the waves of a frozen sea.

The river bed, a cañon cut in the clay, is as level as a table. In places we ride on hard clay, while in others our wheels sink deep into drift sand. The mountains on our right, hundreds of feet high, are formed of stratified sandstone of varying color, from deep red to yellow tints, the different strata running in parallel lines on the face of the rocks.

The vertical sides of the mountains, cut up by arroyos, project in places like round towers close to the river bed. More sloping sides adjoin the projecting buttes.

On a point where the cañon is about one hundred feet wide it is spanned by a wooden bridge. A pier built of logs like a log house, but having two of its corners in the direction of the river, supports the two trusses which rest on either bank. Up to ten or twelve feet above the bed, the logs are covered with grass and brush, an evidence that not long ago, probably last season, the barren waste we are travelling in was a rushing mountain stream ten or twelve feet deep.

We leave the river bed when within a mile or two of the pueblo. A pool of clear water, confined by a dam, here furnished water for our team; and as we get out of the cañon, we see, right before us, an Indian settlement much larger than either Tesuque or San Ildefonso, but of the same general appearance—one and two storied houses on four parallel streets—but with many more houses outside of the pueblo among the fields and trees. Before entering the village we cross an irrigating canal of considerable size, which is fed by the Rio Grande, and furnishes water to a large area around and beyond the village.

On the way we met a number of Indians, squaws and bucks, who had evidently been for supplies to the next American village.

Following a well-beaten road we enter the pueblo from the east. We go down a street, and, on turning to the left, are in front of the main street, which is, no doubt, the original pueblo.

We hitch our horses to a feeding trough, and are immediately surrounded by numbers of children, and are greeted by the old people with their "*como la va*," as one after another comes up to shake hands. Deming, who knew some of the Indians, inquired for Juan Lavater, whom we soon found.

Lavater speaks English well. He has served the United States surveyors as interpreter, and speaks in addition to the Pueblo language, Spanish, Navajo, and Apache. He is well to do ; owns a pair of horses and a good wagon, and is the father of three black-haired youngsters of whom he is exceedingly proud.

When he came over to the carriage with Ed, a tall squaw with a pappoose on her back came with him. I was introduced and shook hands with both, and when I asked Ed whether that tall squaw (she was taller than Juan)

was his wife, he shouted with laughter. "Why," he said, "it is his father-in-law, and the pappoose is Juan's youngest baby."

There I had discovered a new use for fathers-in-law, and I rather rejoiced that I was not a Pueblo Indian, as it did not seem exactly the thing for a gentleman of my age to serve as a nurse-girl for his grandchildren. I saw quite a number of other old men during our stay, who, like Juan's father-in-law, carried the younger generation on their backs. As we were talking to our friend, I took a look up the plaza, and there, coming out of a council house about half-way up, were a troop of Indians walking in single file. They marched to the middle of the square, then turned to the right in the centre, and, marching a short distance, halted. We were just in time to see another spring dance. "We are in luck," I halloed to Ed, who was going with Juan to inspect the quarters he and Carl were to occupy during the night; and, sure enough, we had arrived just in time to witness a performance similar to that we had seen in San Ildefonso. We asked if we could go up to, and near, the place where the dancers had stopped, and were told that we might.

The sight differed slightly from what we had seen. Twenty-five bucks in dancing costume, with three musicians, led by an old, gray-haired man wrapped in a gray blanket, had formed in line in the middle of the square. The old man carried another blanket on his arm. He left the head of the company, and in the centre, close to the line, he spread it on the ground. The three musicians kneeled upon it; each had a large gourd open at the bottom, and with a smaller hole on top, which he laid on the ground. Each had in his left hand a notched stick, and in his right another one, which, when drawn across the notched stick resting on the hollow sphere, produced a deep sound like the pronunciation of a string of letter r's by a Frenchman.

The twenty-five dancers, all ornamented alike, stood facing the musicians. Each dancer wore a breech-clout, held by a broad sash with long tassels nearly touching the ground, and moccasons ornamented with skunk skin; a rattle was in each right hand, and a cottonwood branch in the left. The legs were bare, and painted with white rings; and wide stripes of a white color, which looked not unlike suspenders, went up from the belt, over the shoulders, and down to the fox-skin on the back.

The armlets on the upper arms held bunches of cottonwood, and a wreath of green leaves hung down to the middle of the chest. In place of the head-dresses of cottonwood we had seen before, were eagle feathers fastened to the top of the head.

A funny incident interrupted this stage of the ceremony. A strong breeze was blowing from the west; and one of the ornaments, which had been imperfectly secured, was blown from the head of a dancer. The leader, the old gray-haired Indian, chased it down the plaza until he got the feathers from a youngster who had intercepted their flight. Then he returned to his position behind the musicians, and the dance began.

The musicians draw their sticks, the dancers shake their rattles. The next movement, the dancers turn around and begin to chant. All face the east, as if starting on a march, and commence to lift their feet in unison with the sounds produced by the notched sticks. The tempo increases, and the dancer on the left slowly turns around until he faces the west. As soon as he has completed this motion, the second dancer performs the same movement, and so on through the whole line, till the last Indian has faced about, and has danced there some time.

When the tempo of the music and of the chant changes, the dancer on the right turns slowly till he faces the east again, and one after another all the others change their position. This is repeated again and again, the column first looking to the east, and then to the west, while the leader, who is carefully watching the motions, from time to time corrects some of the performers who are evidently not well enough drilled to please him.

After about twenty minutes the tempo grows gradually slower, and at last the chant and the music cease altogether. The musicians rise, the leader picks up the blanket from the ground, puts it over his left arm, and steps in front of the column. They march away in single file, and about one hundred yards further on the same ceremony is repeated.

"What is the old man who leads the band?" I asked Juan, who stood on my right. "I don't know in English," he answered; but I have no doubt, as he is not the governor of the pueblo, that he is the chief medicine man of the tribe.

San Domingo has over eight hundred inhabitants, and is a much wealthier pueblo than either of those we had visited before, and contentment and thrift appear to be its principal characteristics.

But the dancers and musicians make only a small part of the picture. The whole population have gathered to see the dance. Along the houses in the square, and up on the roofs, the interested spectators in their picturesque dress are lined. But not a smile on any face; all are as sober as if at a church meeting, and yet we have seen them laugh as heartily as white people, when Carl asked the price of the pappoose.

The dance surely had not been prepared expressly for the strangers; it was a relic of the past; and, during the whole performance, I did not see a single Indian who took any notice of the four white men who watched their motions with the greatest attention and interest. It was a picture of unusual brilliancy; the dancers were almost nude, the musicians kneeling on the ground, the spectators on the plaza and on the roofs, dressed in many-colored blankets and dresses. Youngsters and old people, with pappooses tied on their backs, recalled the description of a scene in far-off Japan that I had read some time before, where the young people are actually trained to carry their little brothers and sisters.

It was a bright bit of color, far superior to any I had ever come across in all my travels. San Domingo has three council-houses, exactly like the one we had seen in San Ildefonso, and, as Juan told me, "The old men elect the governor," who is almost an autocrat. "How do you elect the governor?" I asked. "The old men," said Juan, "know best who should be governor, and they select him."

The sun was sinking in the west, and it was time to start, if we wanted to return to Santa Fé that day. A drive of three miles brought us to Wallace, a station on the A. T. & S. F. Railroad, which, as Juan told us, was on the reservation of the San Domingo Indians; and there at six o'clock we found a freight train, which landed my partner and myself in Lamy about eight, and, after waiting for some time, the train on the branch road brought us to Santa Fé about midnight.

The young men stayed at San Domingo over night as guests of Lavater, and they witnessed the next day the erection of a bridge across the Rio Grande, which, had we known about it, we would certainly not have missed, had we to stay a week instead of a single night.

It is no use to cry over spilled milk. I have seen so much that was new and strange, that one scene more or less is of little consequence.

My trip West has opened a new world to me, and it has changed my views of the Indian completely. Grander sights than I had seen can certainly not be found in any part of the globe, and a trip to New Mexico furnishes the same pictures that are seen in Egypt and the East; yet, while hundreds travel to Palestine, few visit the seats of the oldest civilization on the western continent.

To-morrow we start for home, and I will say good-by to Santa Fé and the pueblos, with the hope that I may see them again.

Yours truly,
R. EICKEMEYER.

www.ingramcontent.com/pod-product-compliance
Lightning Source LLC
Chambersburg PA
CBHW022143160426
43197CB00009B/1406